CSS
Pocket Reference

Eric A. Meyer

O'REILLY®

Beijing • Cambridge • Farnham • Köln • Paris • Sebastopol • Taipei • Tokyo

CSS Pocket Reference

by Eric A. Meyer

Copyright © 2001 O'Reilly & Associates, Inc. All rights reserved.
Printed in the United States of America.

Published by O'Reilly & Associates, Inc., 101 Morris Street,
Sebastopol, CA 95472.

Editor: Lorrie LeJeune

Production Editor: Mary Anne Weeks Mayo

Cover Designer: Ellie Volckhausen

Printing History:

> May 2001: First Edition.

0-596-00120-7
[C]

Table of Contents

CSS Pocket Reference

Introduction

Cascading Style Sheets (CSS) is the W3C standard for controlling the visual presentation of web pages. After a short introduction to the key concepts of CSS, this book provides an alphabetical reference to all the CSS1 properties, followed by a chart that details web browser support for CSS.

Rule Structure

A style sheet consists of one or more rules that describe how page elements, which typically correspond to particular HTML tags, should be displayed. Every rule in CSS has two parts, the *selector* and the *declaration*. Figure 1 illustrates the structure of a rule. The selector, on the left side of the rule, specifies the parts of the document to which the style should be applied. In this case, H1 elements are selected. The declaration, on the right side of the rule, is a combination of a CSS *property* and a *value* for that property. In Figure 1, the declaration says that this rule will cause parts of the document to have a color of purple.

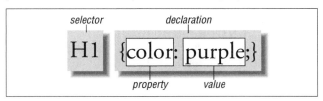

Figure 1. Rule structure

The declaration portion of a CSS rule is always enclosed in curly braces. Each property, which represents a particular stylistic parameter, is separated from its value by a colon (:). Property names in CSS aren't case-sensitive. A declaration can contain several property/value pairs; each such pair must be terminated with a semicolon (;).

Legal values for a property are defined by the property. Some properties take length values, some take color names, and others have a predefined list of accepted values. Some properties even accept multiple keywords, separated by spaces, that together form the value. The "CSS Property Reference" section provides details on the acceptable values for CSS1 properties

Adding Styles to HTML

Style rules can be applied to HTML documents in three ways:

Inline styles

Style information can be specified for an individual element using the style attribute within that element's HTML tag. The value of the style attribute is a standard style declaration without the curly braces:

```
<H1 STYLE="color: purple; font-size: 20pt;">
A large purple heading</H1>
```

Embedded style sheets

A style sheet can be embedded at the top of an HTML document using the STYLE element, which must be placed within the HEAD portion of the document:

```
<HTML><HEAD><TITLE>Stylin!</TITLE>
<STYLE TYPE="text/css">
  H1 {color: purple;}
  P {font-size: 10pt; color: gray;}
</STYLE>
</HEAD>
...
</HTML>
```

External style sheets

Style rules can be stored in a separate text document that is referenced from an HTML document in one of two ways. The first way creates a link to the external style sheet using the LINK tag in the HEAD of the document:

```
<HEAD>
<LINK REL="stylesheet" TYPE="text/css"
HREF="mystyles.css">
</HEAD>
```

The other technique is to import an external style sheet into the STYLE element using the @import directive:

```
<HEAD>
<STYLE TYPE="text/css">
@import url(mystyles.css);
</STYLE>
</HEAD>
```

The @import directive can be combined with other style rules in a STYLE element, as long as the @import line comes before any style rules.

Selectors

Selectors, which identify the elements to which a style applies, come in a variety of forms:

Element selectors

The simplest kind of selector refers to an HTML element by its tag:

```
H1 {color: purple;}
```

Element selectors can be grouped into a comma-separated list, so that a single property applies to all the listed elements:

```
H1, H2, P {color: purple;}
```

Contextual selectors

These selectors specify style attributes for HTML elements based on the context in which they appear. This contextual selector specifies that bold text within a list-item is purple:

```
LI B {color: purple;}
```

With a contextual selector, the individual selectors are separated by whitespace.

Class selectors

Specific HTML elements can be grouped into a class using the CLASS attribute:

```
<H1 CLASS="warning">Danger!</H1>
<P CLASS="warning">Be careful...</P>
```

To specify a style for elements of a particular class, append the class name to the HTML selector, separated by a period (.):

```
H1.warning {color: red;}
```

To apply a style to all elements of a class, regardless of the actual element, omit the tag name:

```
.warning {color: red;}
```

ID selectors

The HTML ID attribute assigns a unique identifier to a particular HTML element:

```
<P ID="first-para">In the beginning...</P>
```

To apply a style to the identified element, simply specify the ID value, preceded by a pound sign (#):

```
#first-para {font-weight: bold;}
```

Psuedo-class and pseudo-element selectors

CSS1 defines some pseudo-classes of the anchor tag (A) to support different styles for various link states. For example, the :visited pseudo-class selects links that have been visited:

```
A:visited {color: red;}
```

Similarly, pseudo-elements are subparts of existing elements for which styles can be specified:

```
P:first-letter {color: red;}
```

Specifying Values

Proper syntax is required for specifying certain kinds of CSS property values. In CSS1, there are five kinds of property values: keywords, length values, percentage values, colors, and URLs. The "CSS Property Reference" section lists the acceptable values for CSS1 properties.

Keywords

Keywords are explicit values, such as `dotted` for `border-style` and `xx-large` for `font-size`. Like property names, keywords aren't case-sensitive.

Length Values

A length value is expressed as a positive or negative number—although some properties accept only positive numbers—followed immediately (no spaces) by a two-letter abbreviation that specifies the units being used. Note that a value of 0 (zero) need not be followed by units. Length units are divided into two types: *absolute units*, which are always measured in the same way, and *relative units*, which are measured in relation to other things. CSS supports the following absolute units:

Inches (`in`)

As you might expect, these are the inches you find on a ruler in the United States. The mapping from inches to a monitor or other display device is usually vague at best, since most systems have no concept of the relation of their display area to real-world measurements such as inches. Thus, inches should be used with extreme caution in screen design.

Centimeters (cm)

The centimeters you find on rulers the world over. There are 2.54 centimeters to an inch, and one centimeter equals 0.394 inches. Centimeters have the same mapping issues as inches.

Millimeters (mm)

There are 10 millimeters to a centimeter, and thus 25.4 millimeters to an inch; 1 millimeter equals 0.0394 inches. Millimeters have the same mapping issues as inches and centimeters.

Points (pt)

Points are a standard typographical measure used by printers, typesetters, and, more recently, word-processing programs. There are 72 points to an inch, so a capital letter of text set to 12 points should be one-sixth of an inch tall. For example, {font-size: 18pt;} is equivalent to {font-size: 0.25in;}, assuming proper mapping of lengths to the display environment.

Picas (pc)

Picas are another unit of typographical measure. A pica is equivalent to 12 points, which means there are 6 picas to an inch. Thus, a capital letter of text set to 1 pica should be a sixth of an inch tall. For example, {font-size: 1.5pc;} should set text to be the same size as the previous point declaration, assuming proper mapping.

CSS supports the following relative units:

Em-height (em)

This refers to the em-height of a given font. In CSS, the em-height is set to be equivalent to the height of the character box for a given font. Ems can set relative sizes for fonts; for example, 1.2em is the same as saying 120%.

X-height (ex)

The x-height of the font describes the height of any lower-case character that doesn't have an ascender (i.e., "d") or a descender (i.e., "p"). The majority of fonts don't include information about their x-height, so most browsers approximate it (badly) by simply setting 1ex to be equal to 0.5em. The exception is IE5/Mac, which attempts to determine the actual x-height of a font by bitmapping an "x" and counting pixels!

Pixels (px)

A pixel is a small onscreen box defined rather abstractly by CSS. In CSS terms, a pixel is defined to be about the size required to yield 90 pixels per inch. Most browsers ignore this in favor of simply addressing the pixels on the monitor. Scaling factors are brought into play when printing, although this can't be relied on.

Percentage Values

A percentage value is specified as a positive or negative number followed by a percent (%) sign and is always computed relative to another value. For example, {line-height: 120%} sets the separation between lines to 120% of the current line height.

Colors

With CSS, there are five ways to specify color values. Four of them involve determining your own mix of red, green, or blue beams; the fifth uses keywords:

#RRGGBB

The hex-pair notation familiar to traditional HTML authors. In this format, the first pair of digits corresponds to the red setting, the second pair to green, and the third pair to blue. Each pair is in hexadecimal notation in the range 00 to FF. Thus, "pure" blue is #0000FF, "pure" red is #FF0000, and so on.

#RGB

A shorter form of the six-digit notation. In this format, each digit is replicated to arrive at an equivalent six-digit value. Thus, #F8C becomes #FF88CC.

rgb(*rrr.rr%,ggg.gg%,bbb.bb%*)

> Specifies RGB values in the range 0% to 100%, with decimal values allowed (e.g., 75.5%). Thus, the value for black is rgb(0%,0%,0%); "pure" blue is rgb(0%,0%,100%).

rgb(*rrr,ggg,bbb*)

> Specifies RGB values in the range 0 to 255. Not coincidentally, this range is the decimal equivalent of 00 to FF in hexadecimal. In this format, "pure" green is rgb(0,255,0), and white is rgb(255,255,255).

keyword

> One of 16 recognized keywords based on the original Windows VGA colors: aqua, black, blue, fuchsia, gray, green, lime, maroon, navy, olive, purple, red, silver, teal, white, and yellow. Browsers may recognize other keywords, but these aren't (as of this writing) found in any specification and aren't guaranteed to work consistently between browsers or indeed from version to version in a single browser.

URLs

URLs aren't often used in style sheets, but when they are, they have the following format:

url(*url*)

> Points to a file, such as a graphic. CSS defines URLs to be relative to the style sheet, but Navigator 4.x interprets URLs relative to the document being styled. Thus, absolute URLs are recommended over relative URLs.

Style Precedence

A single HTML document can import multiple external style sheets, use an embedded style sheet, and specify inline styles. In addition, various style rules can seemingly conflict with each other. CSS uses rules based on document structure, inheritance, specificity, and a cascade order to resolve these conflicts.

The elements in an HTML document form a tree-shaped hierarchy with the HTML element at the top, the HEAD and BODY elements under it, and elements such as H1 and P tags under the BODY branch. In this structure, elements lower in the tree are *descendants* of their *ancestors* higher in the tree. Contextual selectors depend on these structural relationships to operate properly.

CSS uses *inheritance*, which relies on ancestor-descendant relationships, to apply style rules in a document. When a style is applied to a specified element, the style is also applied to the element's descendants, unless there is a more specific style that applies. Note, however, that certain style properties aren't inherited, as detailed in the "CSS Property Reference" section.

Specificity Calculations

Specificity describes the relative weights of various rules. In CSS, more specific rules take precedence over less specific rules. The following chart shows the components that contribute to the specificity value:

Selector Type	Specificity
Element selector	0,0,1
Class and pseudo-class selector	0,1,0
ID selector	1,0,0
!important	Undefined, but higher than the other types of selectors; if two important rules apply to an element, order sorting can determine which rule actually applies

Specificity values are cumulative. Thus, a selector with two element selectors and a class selector has a specificity of (0,1,2), while one element selector, a class selector, and an ID selector add up to (1,1,1). (The values are separated with commas to keep the actual specificity clear.)

Specificity works left to right. Thus, a selector with eleven element selectors (0,0,11) is of lower specificity than a single class selector (0,1,0).

The !important rule can be used to make a particular style more important than other styles of the same specificity:

```
H1 {color: gray !important;}
```

The !important must go at the end of the declaration, right before the semicolon.

The Cascade

The cascade order provides a set of rules for resolving conflicts between different style sheets. Styles with more weight (those defined at a more specific level) take precedence over styles with lower weight. The following steps constitute the cascade:

1. Find all declarations that contain a selector that matches a given element.

2. Sort by explicit weight all declarations applying to given element. Those rules marked !important are given higher weight than those that aren't. Also sort by origin all declarations applying to a given element. There are three origins: author, reader, and user agent (browser). Under normal circumstances, the author's styles override the reader's styles. Important author styles win out over important reader styles in CSS1, but in CSS2, important reader styles are stronger than any other styles. Either author or reader styles override user agent styles.

3. Sort by specificity all declarations applying to a given element. Those elements with a higher specificity have more weight than those with lower specificity.

4. Sort by order all declarations applying to a given element. The later a declaration appears in the style sheet or document, the more weight it's given. Declarations that appear in an imported style sheet come before

all declarations within the stylesheet that imports them, and declarations within STYLE attributes come later than those in the document's embedded style sheet.

Classification of Elements

In CSS, elements are grouped into three types:

Block-level elements
Elements such as paragraphs, headings, lists, tables, DIVs, and BODY. Replaced elements, such as images and form inputs, can be block-level elements but usually aren't. In general, block-level elements are displayed on a line by themselves, beginning on a new line and forcing any element after them to do the same. Block-level elements can be children only of other block-level elements.

Inline elements
Elements such as the anchor element (A), EM, SPAN, and most replaced elements, such as images and form inputs. Inline elements don't force a line break before or after the element. They can be children of any other block, inline, or list-style element.

List-item elements
Elements that in HTML include only the LI element. These are specially defined to have presentation aspects such as a marker (a bullet, letter, or number) and, if within an ordered list, a sense of numerical order. Thus, list-items within such a list can be automatically numbered, based on their context within the document.

Boxes and Borders

All elements in CSS generate a rectangular box called the *element box*. This box describes the amount of space an element and its properties occupy. Figure 2 shows the

---

various components of an element's displayed box. In addition, the following rules apply:

- The background of an element (color or image) extends to the outer edge of the border, thus filling the content area and the padding.

- Only the margins, height, and width may be set to auto. The margins can be given negative lengths, but height and width can't.

- The padding and borders default to 0 (zero) and can't be set to negative lengths.

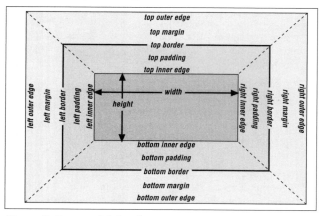

Figure 2. Box model details

Inline Formatting

All elements have a line-height, which has a great deal to do with how inline elements are displayed. The height of a line of text is calculated using the following terms:

Content area
> The box defined by the font-size of each piece of text (whether in an element or not)

Half-leading

The distance determined by the value of `line-height`, where the half-leading equals ((`font-size` - `line-height`)/ 2).

Inline box

The box defined by subtracting the half-leading from the top and bottom of the content area; for any given piece of text, the height of the inline box is always equal to the value of `line-height` for that same text.

Line box

The actual box that is stacked below the previous line box; this bounds the top of the highest inline box and the bottom of the lowest inline box in the line

For each piece of text, an inline box is generated, using the content-area and the half-leading to arrive at its final height. The inline boxes are then aligned according to the value of `vertical-align` for each. Once this is done, the line box is determined. Figure 3 shows the inline box model in more detail.

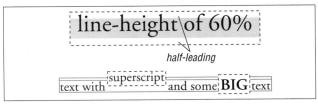

Figure 3. Inline box model details

Float Behavior

Floating allows an element to be positioned against the left or right border, with the text flowing around it. A floated element is placed according to the following rules:

---

1. The left (or right) outer edge of a floated element may not be to the left (or right) of the inner edge of its parent element.

2. The left (or right) outer edge of a floated element must be to the right (or left) of the right (or left) outer edge of a left-floating (or right-floating) element that occurs earlier in the document's source, unless the top of the later element is below the bottom of the former.

3. The right outer edge of a left-floating element may not be to the right of the left outer edge of any right-floating element to its right. The left outer edge of a right-floating element may not be to the left of the right outer edge of any left-floating element to its left.

4. A floating element's top may not be higher than the inner top of its parent.

5. A floating element's top may not be higher than the top of any earlier floating or block-level element.

6. A floating element's top may not be higher than the top of any line box with content that precedes the floating element.

7. A left (or right) floating element that has another floating element to its left (or right) may not have its right outer edge to the right (or left) of its containing block's right (or left) edge.

8. A floating element must be placed as high as possible.

9. A left-floating element must be put as far to the left as possible, a right-floating element as far to the right as possible. A higher position is preferred to one that is further to the right or left.

CSS Property Reference

This reference lists all CSS1 properties, CSS1 pseudo-elements and psuedo-classes, and special declarations. Information about each property includes the property name; its value, if applicable; whether the property is inherited; HTML elements to which the property applies; browser support; a description of how the property works; and examples of how it's used.

The browser support chart shows how CSS is supported in the most popular browsers on the Windows and Macintosh platforms. The browsers are Internet Explorer (Versions 4, 5, and 5.5), Netscape Navigator (Versions 4 and 6), and Opera (Versions 3 and 4). Here is the code:

✓ Supported

✗ Not supported

P Partial support (some values are supported, some aren't)

B Buggy support (anything from a mangled display in the browser window to a browser crash)

Q Quirky support (browser is technically compliant but may not act as expected)

– Not applicable (browser doesn't exist)

:active

Inherited: Yes

Applies to: anchor elements with an HREF attribute

Support:

	IE4	IE5	IE55	NN4	NN6	Op3	Op4
Win	✓	✓	✓	B	✓	✓	✓
Mac	✓	✓	–	✗	✓	–	–

Under CSS1, this pseudo-class applies to hyperlinks but not named anchors. It sets the styles to be used at the moment a hyperlink is selected (e.g., while it's being clicked), and so :active is the CSS replacement for the ALINK attribute on the BODY element in HTML4. In CSS2, other elements can use :active, but the specification doesn't say what they are, and no user agent is known to support :active on any element other than a hyperlink.

Examples:

```
A:active {color: red; background: yellow;}
A.external:active {text-decoration: underline
  overline;}
```

:first-letter

Inherited: Yes

Applies to: Block elements

Support:

	IE4	IE5	IE55	NN4	NN6	Op3	Op4
Win	✗	✗	✓	✗	✓	✓	✓
Mac	✗	✓	–	✗	✓	–	–

Applies styles to the first letter of an element. This pseudo-class can generate drop-cap effects, among other things. The range of properties that can be used with :first-letter is limited to:

- text-decoration
- text-transform
- text-shadow
- line-height
- vertical-align (if float is none)
- float
- clear
- Any font property
- Any color or background property
- Any margin, padding, or border property

IE3 incorrectly applies :first-letter styles to the entire element.

Examples:

```
H1:first-letter {font-size: 125%;}
P:first-letter {color: purple;}
```

:first-line

Inherited: Yes

Applies to: Block elements

Support:

		IE4	IE5	IE55	NN4	NN6	Op3	Op4
	Win	✗	✗	✓	✗	✓	✓	✓
	Mac	✗	✓	–	✗	✓	–	–

Applies styles to the first line of an element. The styles are applied even if the window is resized; the text is simply restyled to encompass only the first line of the element. This can be used to emulate common typographic effects such as larger text in the first line or a change of color. The range of properties that can be used with :first-line is limited to:

- word-spacing
- letter-spacing
- text-decoration
- text-transform
- text-shadow
- vertical-align
- clear
- Any font property
- Any color or background property

IE3 incorrectly applies :first-line styles to the entire element.

Examples:

```
P:first-line {color: red;}
P.lead:first-line {font-size: 150%; font-style:
  italic;}
```

!important

Inherited: Yes

Applies to: Style rules

Support:

		IE4	IE5	IE55	NN4	NN6	Op3	Op4
	Win	✓	✓	✓	✗	✓	✓	✓
	Mac	✗	✓	–	✗	✓	–	–

Style declaration is made important, thereby raising its weight in the cascade. Important declarations override all others. Under CSS1, important author styles override all reader styles, even important ones. In CSS2, this is reversed, so that important reader styles always override the author's styles, important or otherwise.

Examples:

```
H1 {color: maroon !important;}
P.warning {color: rgb(100%,20%,20%); font-weight:bold
  !important;}
/* font-weight is marked important; color is not */
```

:link

Inherited: Yes

Applies to: Anchor elements with an HREF attribute

Support:

	IE4	IE5	IE55	NN4	NN6	Op3	Op4
Win	✓	✓	✓	✓	✓	✓	✓
Mac	✓	✓	–	✓	✓	–	–

This pseudo-class is similar to the HTML attribute Alink. It applies to hyperlinks but not named anchors. Thus, in HTML documents, this pseudo-class may be applied only to A elements with an HREF attribute. :link sets the styles for a hyperlink that points to a URI that hasn't yet been visited (i.e., isn't listed in the browser's history).

Examples:

```
A:link {color: blue;}
A.navigation:link {color: maroon;}
```

:visited

Inherited: Yes

Applies to: Anchor elements with an HREF attribute

Support:

	IE4	IE5	IE55	NN4	NN6	Op3	Op4
Win	✓	✓	✓	B	✓	✓	✓
Mac	✓	✓	–	✗	✓	–	–

This pseudo-class is similar to the HTML attribute vlink. It applies to hyperlinks but not named anchors. Thus, in HTML documents, this pseudo-class may be applied only to A elements with an HREF attribute. :visited sets the styles for a hyperlink that points to a URI that has already been visited (i.e., is listed in the browser's history).

Examples:
```
A:visited {color: navy;}
A.help:visited {color: gray;}
```

---

background

Values:

background-color || *background-image* || *background-repeat*
|| *background-attachment* || *background-position*

Default: Refer to individual properties

Inherited: No

Applies to: All elements

Support:

	IE4	IE5	IE55	NN4	NN6	Op3	Op4
Win	P	✓	✓	P	✓	P	P
Mac	✗	✓	–	P	✓	–	–

A shorthand way of expressing the various background properties using a single rule. Use of this property is encouraged over the other background properties because it's more widely supported and doesn't take as long to type. However, note that using this shorthand property sets *all* background-related property values (e.g., the repeat, position, and so on) to their defaults if they aren't explicitly declared. Thus the following two rules have the same appearance:

```
background: yellow;
background: yellow none top left repeat;
```

Furthermore, these can override previous declarations made with more specific background properties. For example, consider the following rules:

```
H1 {background-repeat: repeat-x;}
H1, H2 {background: yellow url(headback.gif);}
```

In this case, the repeat value for both H1 and H2 elements is set to the default of repeat, overriding the previously declared value of repeat-x. Note that percentage values are allowed for the background-position value.

Navigator 4.x is legendary for its inability to correctly render backgrounds. If there's no border around an element, the background is visible only behind the text of the element, instead of throughout the entire content-area and padding. Unfortunately, if a border is added, there will be a transparent gap between the

---

content-area and the border itself. This isn't the padding, and there's no way to get rid of the gap.

Examples:
```
BODY {background: white url(bg41.gif) fixed center
  repeat-x;}
P {background: url(http://www.pix.org/stone.png) #555;}
PRE {background: yellow;}
```

background-attachment

Values: scroll | fixed

Default: scroll

Inherited: No

Applies to: All elements

Support:

	IE4	IE5	IE55	NN4	NN6	Op3	Op4
Win	✓	✓	✓	✗	✓	✗	✓
Mac	✓	✓	–	✗	✓	–	–

Defines whether or not the background image scrolls along with the element. This is generally applied to BODY only and in fact is largely supported only for that element. It's theoretically possible to create aligned backgrounds in multiple elements using this property; see Chapter 6 of *Cascading Style Sheets: The Definitive Guide* (O'Reilly & Associates) for more details.

Examples:
```
BODY {background-attachment: scroll;}
DIV.fixbg {background-attachment: fixed;}
```

background-color

Values: *color* | transparent

Default: transparent

Inherited: No

Applies to: All elements

Support:

	IE4	IE5	IE55	NN4	NN6	Op3	Op4
Win	✓	✓	✓	B	✓	✓	✓
Mac	✓	✓	–	B	✓	–	–

Sets the background color of an element. The color fills the content area and padding and extends to the outer edge of the element's border. If the border is broken into pieces (e.g., `dashed` or `double`), the background should be visible between the pieces of the border. Not every user agent understands this, however; some take the background to the inner edge of the border or to the midpoint of the border's width.

Navigator 4.x insists on applying the value `transparent` to the parent of an element, not the element itself. This can have the incorrect effect of punching "holes" in the background of the parent element. Opera 4 has a bug that shows up only when a background has been repeated, and the rest of the background of the element is transparent (either by default or when explicitly declared). Scrolling the element offscreen and then bringing it back can cause "holes" to be punched through the repeated images of ancestor elements, thus creating visual anomalies.

Examples:

```
H4 {background-color: white;}
P {background-color: rgb(50%,50%,50%);}
PRE {background-color: background: #FFFF99;}
```

---

background-image

Values: *url* | none

Default: none

Inherited: No

Applies to: All elements

Support:

	IE4	IE5	IE55	NN4	NN6	Op3	Op4
Win	✓	✓	✓	✓	✓	✓	✓
Mac	✓	✓	–	✓	✓	–	–

Sets an image to be the background pattern. Depending on the value of `background-repeat`, the background image may tile indefinitely, only along one axis, or not at all. The starting position of the tiling is defined by the value of `background-position`. Any image the browser can render can be used.

Examples:

```
BODY {background-image: url(bg41.gif);}
H2 {background-image:
  url(http://www.pix.org/dots.png);}
```

---

background-position

Values:

```
[ percentage | length ]{1,2} | [top | center | bottom ] ||
[ left | center | right ]
```

Default: 0% 0%

Inherited: No

Applies to: Block elements and replaced elements

Support:

	IE4	IE5	IE55	NN4	NN6	Op3	Op4
Win	✓	✓	✓	✗	✓	✓	✓
Mac	✓	✓	–	✗	✓	–	–

Sets the starting position of a background image (defined by the value of background-image). background-position sets the origin of the background's tiling or its position if there is no tiling. Percentage values define not only a point within the element but also the same point in the origin image itself, thus allowing (for example) an image to be centered by declaring its position to be 50% 50%. Percentage values also refer to the size of the element itself as well as the size of the origin image. See Chapter 6 of *Cascading Style Sheets: The Definitive Guide* for more details. When percentage or length values are used, the first is always the horizontal position, and the second the vertical. It's possible to mix length and percentage units, but keywords (e.g., top) can't be mixed with either length or percentage units. If only one value is given, it sets the horizontal position, while the missing value is assumed to be either center or 50%. Negative values are permitted. A background image can be positioned outside the element's content area. In this case, only the portion inside the content area is displayed.

Examples:

```
BODY {background-position: top center;}
TD.navbar {background-position: right;}
PRE {background-position: 10px 50%;}
```

background-repeat

Values: repeat | repeat-x | repeat-y | no-repeat

Default: repeat

Inherited: No

Applies to: All elements

Support:

	IE4	IE5	IE55	NN4	NN6	Op3	Op4
Win	P	✓	✓	P	✓	✓	✓
Mac	✓	✓	–	B	✓	–	–

Sets the repeat style for a background image. Note that the axis-related values cause the image repeat in both directions along the specified axis; for example, repeat-x causes tiling to both the right and the left, but not up or down. The repeating of a background image begins with the origin image, whose position is defined by the value of background-position.

IE4/Win repeats only down and to the left. For example, repeat-x causes an image to tile from the origin image to the right but not the left.

Examples:

```
BODY {background-repeat: no-repeat;}
H2 {background-repeat: repeat-x;}
UL {background-repeat: repeat-y;}
```

---

border

Values: *border-width* || *border-style* || *color*

Default: n/a

Inherited: No

Applies to: All elements

Support:

	IE4	IE5	IE55	NN4	NN6	Op3	Op4
Win	P	P	✓	P	✓	P	✓
Mac	P	✓	–	P	✓	–	–

Defines the width, color, and style of the border of an element. Note that while none of the values are required, omitting the border-style value results in no border being visible, since the default value for border-style is none.

Opera doesn't apply border styles to table elements, which is the reason for the P rating. IE4 and Win/IE5 don't apply borders to inline elements, which is the reason for those P ratings.

Examples:

```
H1 {border: 2px dashed olive;}
A:link {border: blue solid 1px;}
P.warning {border: double 5px red;}
```

border-bottom

Values: *border-bottom-width* || *border-style* || *color*

Default: n/a

Inherited: No

Applies to: All elements

Support:

	IE4	IE5	IE55	NN4	NN6	Op3	Op4
Win	P	P	✓	✗	✓	P	✓
Mac	P	✓	−	✗	✓	−	−

Defines the width, color, and style of the bottom border of an element. The usual caveats about border-style apply.

Opera doesn't apply border styles to table elements, which is the reason for the P rating. IE4 and IE5/Win don't apply borders to inline elements, which is the reason for those P ratings.

Examples:

```
UL {border-bottom: 0.5in groove green;}
A:active {border-bottom: purple 2px dashed;}
```

border-bottom-width

Values: thin | medium | thick | *length*

Default: medium

Inherited: No

Applies to: All elements

Support:

	IE4	IE5	IE55	NN4	NN6	Op3	Op4
Win	P	P	✓	B	✓	✓	✓
Mac	P	✓	−	B	✓	−	−

Sets the width of the bottom border of an element. Negative length values aren't permitted. The usual caveats about border-style apply.

With block elements, Navigator 4.x creates visible borders even when no border-style is set (the default should be no border) and doesn't set borders on all sides when a style is set. Things get really ugly with inline elements; you must avoid inline element borders if writing for NN4. IE4 and IE5/Win correctly handle borders on block-level elements but ignore them for inlines.

Examples:

```
UL {border-bottom-width: 0.5in;}
A:active {border-bottom-width: 2px;}
```

border-color

Values: *color*{1,4}

Default: The value of color for the element itself

Inherited: No

Applies to: All elements

Support:

	IE4	IE5	IE55	NN4	NN6	Op3	Op4
Win	✓	✓	✓	P	✓	✓	✓
Mac	✓	✓	–	P	✓	–	–

Sets the color of the overall border of an element. It's possible to set a different color for each side by listing them in the order top-right-bottom-left.

Navigator 4.x and Opera 3.6 don't set colors on individual sides, as in border-color: red blue green purple. IE4 and Win/IE5 can't apply border colors to inline elements, since they don't apply borders to inlines, but this isn't penalized here.

Examples:

```
H1 {border-color: purple;}
A:visited {border-color: maroon;}
```

border-left

Values: *border-left-width* || *border-style* || *color*

Default: n/a

Inherited: No

Applies to: All elements

	IE4	IE5	IE55	NN4	NN6	Op3	Op4
Win	P	P	✓	✗	✓	P	✓
Mac	P	✓	–	✗	✓	–	–

Defines the width, color, and style of the left border of an element. The usual caveats about border-style apply.

Opera doesn't apply border styles to table elements, which is the reason for the P rating. IE4 and Win/IE5 don't apply borders to inline elements.

Examples:

```
P {border-left: 3em solid gray;}
PRE {border-left: double black 4px;}
```

---

border-left-width

Values: thin | medium | thick | *length*

Default: medium

Inherited: No

Applies to: All elements

Support:

	IE4	IE5	IE55	NN4	NN6	Op3	Op4
Win	P	P	✓	B	✓	✓	✓
Mac	P	✓	–	B	✓	–	–

Sets the width of the left border of an element, which inherits the element's background and may have a foreground of its own (see border-style). Negative length values aren't permitted. The usual caveats about border-style apply.

Navigator creates visible borders even when no border-style is set and doesn't set borders on all sides when a style is set. Things get really ugly when borders are applied to inline styles. IE4 and Win/IE5 correctly handle borders on block-level elements but ignore them for inlines.

Examples:

```
P {border-left-width: 3em;}
PRE {border-left-width: 4px;}
```

---

border-right

Values: *border-right-width* || *border-style* || *color*

Default: n/a

Inherited: No

Applies to: All elements

Support:

	IE4	IE5	IE55	NN4	NN6	Op3	Op4
Win	P	P	✓	✗	✓	P	✓
Mac	P	✓	–	✗	✓	–	–

Defines the width, color, and style of the right border of an element. The usual caveats about border-style apply.

Opera doesn't apply border styles to table elements, which is the reason for the P rating. IE4 and IE5 don't apply borders to inline elements.

Examples:

```
IMG {border-right: 30px dotted blue;}
H3 {border-right: cyan 1em inset;}
```

border-right-width

Values: thin | medium | thick | *length*

Default: medium

Inherited: No

Applies to: All elements

Support:

	IE4	IE5	IE55	NN4	NN6	Op3	Op4
Win	P	P	✓	B	✓	✓	✓
Mac	P	✓	–	B	✓	–	–

Sets the width of the right border of an element, which inherits the element's background and may have a foreground of its own (see border-style). Negative length values aren't permitted. The usual caveats about border-style apply.

Navigator 4.x creates visible borders even when no border-style is set and doesn't set borders on all side when a style is set. Things get really ugly when borders are applied to inline styles. IE4 and Win/IE5 correctly handle borders on block-level elements but ignore them for inlines.

Examples:

```
IMG {border-right-width: 30px;}
H3 {border-right-width: 1em;}
```

border-style

Values:

none | dotted | dashed | solid | double | groove | ridge |
inset | outset

Default: none

Inherited: No

Applies to: All elements

Support:

	IE4	IE5	IE55	NN4	NN6	Op3	Op4
Win	P	P	✓	P	✓	✓	✓
Mac	✓	✓	–	P	✓	–	–

Sets the style of the overall border of an element, using either the
color set by border-color or the foreground of the element itself if
no border-color has been defined. Note that setting the border-
style to none (its default value) results in no border at all. In this
case, any value of border-width is ignored, and the width of the
border set to zero. CSS1 doesn't require recognition of any values
besides none and solid. Any unrecognized value from the list of
values should be reinterpreted as solid.

Navigator 4.x doesn't reset the border-width to zero if border-
style is none, but instead incorrectly honors the width setting.

Examples:

```
H1 {border-style: solid;}
IMG {border-style: inset;}
```

border-top

Values: *border-top-width* || *border-style* || *color*

Default: n/a

Inherited: No

Applies to: All elements

Support:

	IE4	IE5	IE55	NN4	NN6	Op3	Op4
Win	P	P	✓	✗	✓	P	✓
Mac	P	✓	–	✗	✓	–	–

Defines the width, color, and style of the top border of an element.
The usual caveats about border-style apply.

Opera doesn't apply border styles to table elements, which is the reason for the P rating. IE4 and Win/IE5 don't apply borders to inline elements.

Examples:

```
UL {border-top: 0.5in solid black;}
H1 {border-top: dashed 1px gray;}
```

---

border-top-width

Values: thin | medium | thick | *length*

Default: medium

Inherited: No

Applies to: All elements

Support:

	IE4	IE5	IE55	NN4	NN6	Op3	Op4
Win	P	P	✓	B	✓	✓	✓
Mac	P	✓	–	B	✓	–	–

Sets the width of the top border of an element. Negative length values aren't permitted. The usual caveats about border-style apply.

Navigator creates visible borders even when no border-style is set and doesn't set borders on all sides when a style is set. Things get really ugly when borders are applied to inline styles. IE4 and Win/IE5 correctly handle borders on block-level elements but ignore them for inlines.

Examples:

```
UL {border-top-width: 0.5in;}
H1 {border-top-width: 1px;}
```

---

border-width

Values: [thin | medium | thick | *length*]{1,4}

Default: n/a

Inherited: No

Applies to: All elements

Support:

	IE4	IE5	IE55	NN4	NN6	Op3	Op4
Win	P	P	✓	B	✓	✓	✓
Mac	P	✓	–	B	✓	–	–

Sets the width of the overall border of an element, which inherits the element's background and may have a foreground of its own (see border-style). Negative length values aren't permitted. The usual caveats about border-style apply.

Navigator creates visible borders even when no border-style is set and doesn't set borders on all side when a style is set. Things get really ugly when borders are applied to inline styles. IE4 and Win/IE5 correctly handle borders on block-level elements but ignore them for inlines.

Examples:

```
H1 {border-width: 2ex;}
IMG {border-width: 5px;}
```

---

clear

Values: none | left | right | both

Default: none

Inherited: No

Applies to: All elements

Support:

	IE4	IE5	IE55	NN4	NN6	Op3	Op4
Win	P	P	✓	P	✓	B	✓
Mac	✓	✓	–	P	✓	–	–

Defines the sides of an element on which no floating images may be placed. The effect of this is to move the element down until the top of its border-edge is below the bottom edge of the floated element. This downward movement is technically accomplished by increasing the top margin of the element until its top border is lower than the bottom of the floated element.

Like float, clear isn't simple to support. There is typically basic support, but as things get more complicated, browser behavior tends to break down. Thoroughly test pages using this property.

Examples:

```
H1 {clear: both;}
H3 {clear: right;}
```

---

color

Values: *color*

Default: Browser specific

Inherited: Yes

Applies to: All elements

Support:

	IE4	IE5	IE55	NN4	NN6	Op3	Op4
Win	✓	✓	✓	✓	✓	✓	✓
Mac	✓	✓	–	✓	✓	–	–

Sets the foreground color of a given element. For text, this sets the text color; for bitmap images such as GIF and JPG, it has no effect. The value of color is assumed by any borders of an element, unless they have had a color explicitly set using border-color. In the three-digit hex format, each digit is replicated; thus, #0F0 is the same as #00FF00.

Examples:

```
STRONG {color: rgb(255,128,128);}
H3 {color: navy;}
P.warning {color: #FF0000;}
PRE.pastoral {color: #0F0;}
```

---

display

Values: block | inline | list-item | none

Default: block

Inherited: No

Applies to: All elements

Support:

	IE4	IE5	IE55	NN4	NN6	Op3	Op4
Win	P	P	P	P	✓	P	✓
Mac	P	✓	–	P	✓	–	–

Classifies elements into broad categories. The most popular value is probably none, which surpresses the display of an element altogether. Gratuitous use of display with a document type such as HTML can be dangerous, since HTML already has a display hierarchy defined, and so in these circumstances the use of display is strongly discouraged. However, in the case of XML, which has no

---

such hierarchy, `display` is indispensable. In CSS2, the range of values for `display` is expanded but not well supported.

Opera 3.6 almost gets `inline` right but seems to honor the occasional carriage return as though it were a `<BR>` element, instead of plain whitespace.

Examples:

```
.hide {display: none;}
LI {display: list-item;}
H1 {display: block;}
IMG {display: inline;}
```

---

float

Values: `left` | `right` | `none`

Default: none

Inherited: No

Applies to: All elements

Support:

	IE4	IE5	IE55	NN4	NN6	Op3	Op4
Win	P	P	Q	P	✓	B	Q
Mac	B	Q	–	P	✓	–	–

Sets the float direction for an element. This is generally applied to images to allow text to flow around them, but under CSS1, any element may be floated. Note that, for elements such as paragraphs, floating the element causes its width to tend toward zero unless an explicit width is assigned; thus, width assignment is a crucial part of floating any non-replaced element.

`float` is one of the most complicated and hardest-to-implement aspects of the entire specification. Basic floating is generally supported by all browsers, especially on images, but when the specification is closely tested, or the document structure becomes complicated, floating is most often used incorrectly or not at all. The floating of text elements is especially inconsistent, although IE5 and Opera have cleaned up their act to a large degree, leaving WinIE4 and Nav4 the major transgressors in this respect. You should use `float` carefully and thoroughly test any pages employing it.

Opera 4 seems to place floated elements a bit off from where the ideal place would seem to be, but in general, its support is extremely robust and can generally be counted on.

Examples:

```
IMG.figure {float: left;}
P.sidebar {float: right; width: 15em;}
```

---

font

Values:

> [*font-style* || *font-variant* || *font-weight*]? *font-size*
> [/ *line-height*]? *font-family*

Default: Refer to individual properties

Inherited: Yes

Applies to: All elements

Support:

	IE4	IE5	IE55	NN4	NN6	Op3	Op4
Win	P	P	✓	P	✓	✓	✓
Mac	Q	✓	–	P	✓	–	–

A shorthand property for the other font properties. Any values may be omitted except for font-size and font-family, which are always required for a valid font declaration and must appear in that order. Note the incorrect examples shown.

Examples:

```
P {font: small-caps italic bold 12pt/14pt
  Helvetica,sans-serif;}
P.wrong {font: bold Helvetica,sans-serif;} /* missing a
  font-size */
P.wrong {font: 12pt Times,serif bold;} /* font-weight
  must come before the others */
P.wrong {font: 12pt italic Times;} /* font-style must
  come before font-size */
P.valid {font: 14pt Arial;} /* technically correct,
  although generic font-families are encouraged for
  fallback purposes */
```

---

font-family

Values:

> [[*family-name* | *generic-family*],]* [*family-name* |
> *generic-family*]

Default: Browser specific

Inherited: Yes

Applies to: All elements

Support:

	IE4	IE5	IE55	NN4	NN6	Op3	Op4
Win	✓	✓	✓	✓	✓	✓	✓
Mac	✓	✓	–	✓	✓	–	–

Declares a specific font to be used, a generic font family, or both. Values for a generic font family are serif, sans-serif, monospace, cursive, and fantasy. If a font name contains whitespace, it must be enclosed with either single- or double-quotation marks. Note that the use of a specific font family is dependent on the user having that font installed on his system. So using generic font families is strongly encouraged, since this causes the user agent to try substituting a similar font. The fantasy and cursive font families are especially problematic, and it's recommended you avoid using either one. See Chapter 5 of *Cascading Style Sheets: The Definitive Guide* for more information about font families.

Examples:

```
P {font-family: Helvetica, Arial, sans-serif;}
LI {font-family: Times, TimesNR, "New Century
  Schoolbook", serif;}
PRE {font-family: Courier, "Courier New", "Andale
  Mono", Monaco, monospace;}
```

---

font-size

Values:

```
xx-small | x-small | small | medium | large | x-large |
xx-large | larger | smaller | length | percentage
```

Default: medium

Inherited: Yes

Applies to: All elements

Support:

	IE4	IE5	IE55	NN4	NN6	Op3	Op4
Win	P	P	P	✗	✓	✓	✓
Mac	Q	✓	–	✗	✓	–	–

Sets the size of the font. This can be defined as an absolute size, a relative size, a length value, or a percentage value. Percentage values are relative to parent element's font size. Negative length and percentage values aren't permitted. The dangers of font-size

---

assignment are many and varied, and points are particularly discouraged in web design, as there's no certain relationship between points and the pixels on a monitor. Note also that, due to early misunderstandings, setting the `font-size` to `medium` leads to different results in Internet Explorer and Navigator 4.x. Some of these problems are covered in Chapter 5 of *Cascading Style Sheets: The Definitive Guide*; for further discussion, refer to *http://style.cleverchimp.com/*. For best results, you should use either percentages or em units for font sizing. As a last resort, pixel sizes can be used, but this approach has serious accessibility penalties because it prevents users from resizing text, even if it's too small for them to read comfortably.

IE4/5's values for absolute sizes assigns `small` to be the same size as unstyled text, instead of `medium`, as you might expect. Thus, declaring an absolute font size (such as `font-size: medium`) will almost certainly lead to different font sizes in Navigator and Explorer. Navigator 4.x is more in line with the intent of the CSS specification, while Explorer's behavior has a solid foundation in traditional HTML rendering.

Examples:

```
H2 {font-size: 200%;}
CODE {font-size: 0.9em;}
P.caption {font-size: 9px;}
```

---

font-style

Values: normal | italic | oblique

Default: normal

Inherited: Yes

Applies to: All elements

Support:

	IE4	IE5	IE55	NN4	NN6	Op3	Op4
Win	✓	✓	✓	P	✓	✓	✓
Mac	✓	✓	–	P	✓	–	–

Sets the font to use either italic, oblique, or normal text. Italic text is generally a defined font face within the font itself, whereas oblique text is less often so. In the latter case, the user agent can compute a slanted font face. However, the reality is that user agents rarely recognize the difference between italic and oblique text and almost always render both in exactly the same way.

Examples:

```
EM {font-style: oblique;}
I {font-style: italic;}
```

font-variant

Values: normal | small-caps

Default: normal

Inherited: Yes

Applies to: All elements

Support:

	IE4	IE5	IE55	NN4	NN6	Op3	Op4
Win	Q	Q	Q	✗	✓	✓	✓
Mac	Q	✓	–	✗	✓	–	–

This currently has two values: small-caps and normal. The small-caps variant can either be applied as a face of the selected font or computed by the user agent. Under the rules of CSS, user agents can claim support for small-caps by simply uppercasing all the letters. Since this isn't typically what you'd expect, user agents that do this are marked as having Quirky support.

Examples:

```
H3 {font-variant: small-caps;}
P {font-variant: normal;}
```

font-weight

Values:

```
normal | bold | bolder | lighter | 100 | 200 | 300 | 400 |
500 | 600 | 700 | 800 | 900
```

Default: normal

Inherited: Yes

Applies to: All elements

Support:

	IE4	IE5	IE55	NN4	NN6	Op3	Op4
Win	✓	✓	✓	P	✓	✓	✓
Mac	✓	✓	–	P	✓	–	–

Sets the weight of a font, making it heavier or lighter. The numeric value 400 is equivalent to the value normal, and 700 is equal to bold. Each numeric value is at least as heavy as the next-lower value, and at least as light as the next-higher number. Thus, if a font has only two weights—normal and bold—the numbers 100 through 500 are normal, and 600 through 900 are bold.

Examples:

```
B {font-weight: 700;}
STRONG {font-weight: bold;}
.delicate {font-weight; lighter;}
```

height

Values: *length* | auto

Default: auto

Inherited: No

Applies to: Block level elements and replaced elements

Support:

	IE4	IE5	IE55	NN4	NN6	Op3	Op4
Win	✓	✓	✓	✗	✓	✓	✓
Mac	✓	✓	–	✗	✓	–	–

Sets the height of an element. height is most often applied to images but can be used on any block-level or replaced element, although support for such behavior isn't widespread as of this writing. In fact, CSS1 states that a user agent can treat any value as auto when height is applied to non-replaced elements such as paragraphs. Negative length values aren't permitted.

Examples:

```
IMG.icon {height: 50px;}
```

letter-spacing

Values: normal | *length*

Default: normal

Inherited: Yes

Applies to: All elements

Support:

	IE4	IE5	IE55	NN4	NN6	Op3	Op4
Win	✓	✓	✓	✗	✓	✓	✓
Mac	✓	✓	–	✗	✓	–	–

Sets the amount of whitespace between letters. A letter is defined as any displayed character, including numbers, symbols, and other font glyphs. Length values can define a modifier to the usual spacing, not the entire space itself; thus, `normal` is synonymous with 0 (zero). Negative values are permitted and cause letters to kern (bunch closer together).

Examples:

```
P.spacious {letter-spacing: 6px;}
EM {letter-spacing: 0.2em;}
P.cramped {letter-spacing: -0.5em;}
```

line-height

Values: normal | *number* | *length* | *percentage*

Default: normal

Inherited: Yes

Applies to: All elements

Percentage values: Relative to the font size of the element itself

Support:

	IE4	IE5	IE55	NN4	NN6	Op3	Op4
Win	✓	✓	✓	P	✓	Q	✓
Mac	✓	✓	–	P	✓	–	–

Sets the intrinsic height of any non-replaced element. (See the section on inline formatting at the beginning of the book for a more detailed explanation of `line-height`.) The difference between the value of `line-height` and the value of `font-size` is called *leading*, and half of the leading (otherwise known as half-leading) is applied above and below the content of an element or line of text. Negative values aren't permitted. Using a number defines a scaling factor that is multiplied by the `font-size`, and the number itself is inherited, not the computed value. This allows for more intelligent page layout and is strongly preferred over other methods of setting `line-height`. The drawback to using a number value is that IE3 interprets it as a number of pixels.

For inline elements, Opera 3.6 applies background colors to the space between lines, as opposed to just the text itself, when the background is set for an inline element within the text. (See the CSS1 Test Suite for more details.)

Navigator 4.x incorrectly permits negative values for this property.

Examples:

```
P {line-height: 1.5em;}
H2 {line-height: 200%;}
UL {line-height: 1.2;}
PRE {line-height: 0.75em;}
```

list-style

Values:

```
list-style-type || list-style-position ||
list-style-image
```

Default: n/a

Inherited: Yes

Applies to: List elements

Support:

	IE4	IE5	IE55	NN4	NN6	Op3	Op4
Win	P	✓	✓	P	✓	✓	✓
Mac	P	✓	–	P	✓	–	–

A shorthand property condensing all other list-style properties. It applies to all elements with a display value of list-item; in ordinary HTML, this is any <LI> element. If an image isn't available or can't be rendered, the value for list-style-type is used for the bullets.

Examples:

```
UL {list-style: square url(bullet3.gif) outer;}
  /* values are inherited to LI elements */
OL {list-style: upper-roman;}
```

list-style-image

Values: *url* | none

Default: none

Inherited: Yes

Applies to: List elements

Support:

	IE4	IE5	IE55	NN4	NN6	Op3	Op4
Win	✓	✓	✓	✗	✓	✓	✓
Mac	✓	✓	–	✗	✓	–	–

Declares an image that is used as the bullet in an unordered or ordered list. This style applies to elements with a display value of list-item (e.g., <LI> elements). The position of the image with respect to the content of the list-item is defined using list-style-position. If the declared image isn't available or can't be rendered, the value for list-style-type is used for the bullets.

Examples:
```
UL {list-style-image: url(bullet3.gif);}
UL LI {list-style-image:
  url(http://my.web.site/pix/sun.png);}
```

list-style-position

Values: inside | outside

Default: outside

Inherited: Yes

Applies to: List elements

Support:

	IE4	IE5	IE55	NN4	NN6	Op3	Op4
Win	✓	✓	✓	✗	✓	✓	✓
Mac	✓	✓	–	✗	✓	–	–

Declares the position of the bullet or number in an unordered or ordered list with respect to the content of the list-item. The default value mimics traditional HTML renderings of lists, while inside places the bullet as if it were the first character in the list-item's content. If the bullet is set to be outside, it's placed in the margin of the list-item element. The exact behavior in this circumstance isn't defined in CSS.

The positioning and formatting of list-items when set to this value are a bit odd under IE4/Mac.

Examples:
```
LI {list-style-position: outside;}
OL LI {list-style-position: inside;}
```

list-style-type

Values:
```
disc | circle | square | decimal | lower-roman |
upper-roman | lower-alpha | upper-alpha | none
```

Default: `disc`

Inherited: Yes

Applies to: List elements

Support:

	IE4	IE5	IE55	NN4	NN6	Op3	Op4
Win	✓	✓	✓	✓	✓	✓	✓
Mac	✓	✓	–	P	✓	–	–

Declares the type of bullet numbering system to be used in either an unordered or ordered list, depending on the value specified. CSS2 add many more values with international flavor (e.g., `hebrew` and `armenian`), but as of this writing, they aren't widely supported. There is no defined behavior for what happens when a list using an alphabetic ordering exceeds the letters in the list. For example, once an `upper-latin` list reaches Z, the specification doesn't say what the next bullet should be.

Navigator 4.x displays question marks for bullets when using the value `none`.

Examples:

```
UL {list-style-type: square;}
OL {list-style-type: lower-roman;}
```

---

margin

Values: [*length* | *percentage* | auto]{1,4}

Default: n/a

Inherited: No

Applies to: All elements

Support:

	IE4	IE5	IE55	NN4	NN6	Op3	Op4
Win	P	P	✓	B	✓	✓	B
Mac	P	✓	–	B	✓	–	–

Sets the size of the overall margin of an element. Vertically adjacent margins of block-level elements are collapsed to be as large as the largest margin, whereas inline elements effectively don't take top and bottom margins (they are allowed but have no effect on page layout). With inline elements, only the left and right margins of inline elements have an effect, and they don't collapse with adjacent margins. Margins set on floated elements aren't collapsed with other margins under any circumstance. Negative values are permitted, but caution is recommended, as these can cause

---

elements to overwrite other parts of a page or to appear wider than their parent elements. Percentage values of `margin` refer to the width of the closest block-level ancestor.

All margin properties seem to be problematic, or else completely unsupported, on inline elements. In the case of `margin`, support is pretty good on block-level elements in IE4/Win and IE5/Win, while with inline elements, IE4/Win and IE5/Win ignore this property completely. IE5/Mac correctly honors margins on all elements. Navigator 4.x does fairly well so long as margins aren't applied to floating or inline elements, in which case major bugs can be tripped.

Opera 4's problems with correctly applying right and left margins to inline elements seem to get worse if you use the `margin` shorthand property.

Examples:

```
H1 {margin: 2ex;}
P {margin: auto;}
IMG {margin: 10px;}
```

---

margin-bottom

Values: *length* | *percentage* | auto

Default: 0

Inherited: No

Applies to: All elements

Support:

	IE4	IE5	IE55	NN4	NN6	Op3	Op4
Win	P	P	✓	✗	✓	✓	✓
Mac	P	✓	–	✗	✓	–	–

Sets the size of the bottom margin of an element. Negative values are permitted, but caution is recommended as that can pull following elements up, possibly overwriting some or all elements with the negative margin. Bottom margins on inline elements have no effect on document layout. Percentage values of `margin-bottom` refer to the width of the closest block-level ancestor.

All margin properties seem to be problematic, or else completely unsupported, on inline elements; see `margin` for details.

Examples:

```
UL {margin-bottom: 0.5in;}
H1 {margin-bottom: 2%;}
```

---

margin-left

Values: *length* | *percentage* | auto

Default: 0

Inherited: No

Applies to: All elements

Support:

	IE4	IE5	IE55	NN4	NN6	Op3	Op4
Win	P	P	✓	B	✓	✓	B
Mac	P	✓	–	B	✓	–	–

Sets the size of the left margin of an element. Negative values are permitted, but caution is recommended, as they can cause the left edge of the element to push outside the left edge of the parent element(s). Percentage values of margin-left refer to width of the closest block-level ancestor.

All margin properties seem to be problematic, or else completely unsupported, on inline elements; see margin for details. Opera 4 sometimes applies left margins to all the boxes of an inline element, not just the first one. This seems to come and go somewhat randomly, but it's common enough to be easily noticeable.

Examples:

```
P {margin-left: 5%;}
PRE {margin-left: 3em;}
```

---

margin-right

Values: *length* | *percentage* | auto

Default: 0

Inherited: No

Applies to: All elements

Support:

	IE4	IE5	IE55	NN4	NN6	Op3	Op4
Win	P	P	Q	B	B	✓	B
Mac	P	✓	–	B	B	–	–

Sets the size of the right margin of an element. Negative values are permitted, but caution is recommended, as they can cause the right edge of the element to push outside the right edge of the parent element(s). Percentage values of `margin-right` refer to width of the closest block-level ancestor.

All margin properties seem to be problematic, or else completely unsupported, on inline elements; see `margin` for details. Opera 4 sometimes applies right margins to all the boxes of an inline element, not just the last one. This seems to come and go somewhat randomly, but it's common enough to be easily noticeable. As of this writing, Netscape 6 has a specific bug relating to right margins on inline elements and line-breaking.

Examples:

```
IMG {margin-right: 30px;}
OL {margin-right: 5em;}
```

---

margin-top

Values: *length* | *percentage* | auto

Default: 0

Inherited: No

Applies to: All elements

Support:

	IE4	IE5	IE55	NN4	NN6	Op3	Op4
Win	P	P	✓	P	✓	✓	B
Mac	P	✓	–	P	✓	–	–

Sets the size of the top margin of an element. Negative values are permitted, but caution is recommended, as they can pull the element up into preceding elements, possibly overwriting some or all of the preceding elements. Top margins on inline elements have no effect on document layout. Percentage values of `margin-top` refer to the width of the closest block-level ancestor.

All margin properties seem to be problematic, or else completely unsupported, on inline elements; see `margin` for details.

Examples:

```
UL {margin-top: 0.5in;}
H3 {margin-top: 1.5em;}
```

padding

Values: [*length* | *percentage*]{1,4}

Default: n/a

Inherited: No

Applies to: All elements

Support:

	IE4	IE5	IE55	NN4	NN6	Op3	Op4
Win	P	P	Q	B	✓	B	✓
Mac	P	✓	–	B	✓	–	–

Sets the size of the overall padding of an element. The padding uses the element's background; in other words, the background of an element fills its content area and padding. Padding set on inline elements doesn't affect line-height calculations but is applied to the right and left ends of the element. If an inline element has both padding and a background, the background may be extended above and below the edges of the line-box in which the inline element appears, but user agents aren't required to support this behavior. There's also no defined behavior to say whether the foreground content of a previous line appears above the background of a succeeding line or is overwritten by that background. Negative values aren't permitted. Percentage values of padding refer to width of the closest block-level ancestor.

All padding properties seem to be problematic, or else completely unsupported, on inline elements. Opera 3.6 correctly ignores negative padding values but will alter the line-height based on values of padding applied to inline elements, which is incorrect. IE4/Win and IE5/Win honor padding assignments on block-level elements but not inline elements. Navigator 4.x does fairly well as long as padding isn't applied to floating or inline elements, in which case major bugs can be tripped.

Examples:

```
H1 {padding: 2ex;}
IMG {padding: 10px;}
```

padding-bottom

Values: *length* | *percentage*

Default: 0

Inherited: No

Applies to: All elements

Percentage values: Refer to width of closest block-level ancestor

Support:

	IE4	IE5	IE55	NN4	NN6	Op3	Op4
Win	P	P	✓	B	✓	✓	✓
Mac	P	✓	–	B	✓	–	–

Sets the size of the bottom padding of an element. This padding uses the element's background, if one has been set. Negative values aren't permitted. Percentage values of `padding-bottom` refer to the width of the closest block-level ancestor.

All padding properties seem to be problematic, or else completely unsupported, on inline elements; see `padding` for details.

Examples:

```
UL {padding-bottom: 0.5in;}
H1 {padding-bottom: 2%;}
```

---

padding-left

Values: *length* | *percentage*

Default: 0

Inherited: No

Applies to: All elements

Support:

	IE4	IE5	IE55	NN4	NN6	Op3	Op4
Win	P	P	✓	B	✓	✓	✓
Mac	P	✓	–	B	✓	–	–

Sets the size of the left padding of an element. This padding uses the element's background, if one has been set. Negative values aren't permitted. Percentage values of `padding-left` refer to width of the closest block-level ancestor.

All padding properties seem to be problematic, or else completely unsupported, on inline elements; see `padding` for details.

Examples:

```
P {padding-left: 5%;}
PRE {padding-left: 3em;}
```

padding-right

Values: *length* | *percentage*

Default: 0

Inherited: No

Applies to: All elements

Support:

	IE4	IE5	IE55	NN4	NN6	Op3	Op4
Win	P	P	Q	B	✓	✓	✓
Mac	P	✓	–	B	✓	–	–

Sets the size of the right padding of an element. This padding uses the element's background, if one has been set. Negative values aren't permitted. Percentage values of padding-right refer to width of the closest block-level ancestor.

All padding properties seem to be problematic, or else completely unsupported, on inline elements; see padding for details.

Examples:

```
IMG {padding-right: 30px;}
OL {padding-right: 5em;}
```

padding-top

Values: *length* | *percentage*

Default: 0

Inherited: No

Applies to: All elements

Support:

	IE4	IE5	IE55	NN4	NN6	Op3	Op4
Win	P	P	Q	B	✓	✓	✓
Mac	P	✓	–	B	✓	–	–

Sets the size of the top padding of an element. This padding uses the element's background, if one has been set. Negative values aren't permitted. Percentage values of padding-top refer to width of the closest block-level ancestor.

All padding properties seem to be problematic, or else completely unsupported, on inline elements; see padding for details.

Examples:

```
UL {padding-top: 0.5in;}
H3 {padding-top: 1.5em;}
```

text-align

Values: left | right | center | justify

Default: Browser specific

Inherited: Yes

Applies to: Block

Support:

	IE4	IE5	IE55	NN4	NN6	Op3	Op4
Win	✓	✓	✓	✓	✓	✓	✓
Mac	P	✓	–	P	✓	–	–

Sets the horizontal alignment of the text in an element, or more precisely, defines to which side of the element's content area the line boxes are aligned. The value justify is supported by programatically adjusting the letter- and word-spacing of the line's content; results may vary by user agent.

In Navigator 4.x, justify can break down in tables but generally works in other circumstances.

Examples:

```
P {text-align: justify;}
H4 {text-align: center;}
```

text-decoration

Values:
none | [underline || overline || line-through || blink]

Default: none

Inherited: No

Applies to: All elements

Support:

	IE4	IE5	IE55	NN4	NN6	Op3	Op4
Win	P	P	P	Q	B	P	P
Mac	P	P	–	Q	B	–	–

Sets certain effects on the text, such as underline and blink. User agents aren't required to support blink. These decorations span child elements that don't have text decoration defined; see Chapter 4 of *Cascading Style Sheets: The Definitive Guide* for more details. Combinations of the values are legal. When two `text-decoration` rules apply to the same element, the values of the two rules aren't combined. For example:

```
H1 {text-decoration: overline;}
H1, H2 {text-decoration: underline;}
```

Given these styles, H1 elements are underlined with no overline, because the value of `overline` completely overrides the value of `underline`. If H1s have both overlines and underlines, use the value `overline underline` for the H1 rule.

In practice, setting an inline element's `text-decoration` to `none` turns off all decorations, regardless of the parent's decoration. The only exception to this is Opera, which implements the specification correctly—except Opera 4, which doesn't span inline images with the text decoration of a parent element.

Examples:

```
U {text-decoration: underline;}
.old {text-decoration: line-through;}
U.old {text-decoration: line-through underline;}
```

---

text-indent

Values: *length | percentage*

Default: 0

Inherited: Yes

Applies to: Block

Support:

	IE4	IE5	IE55	NN4	NN6	Op3	Op4
Win	P	P	✓	B	✓	✓	B
Mac	P	✓	–	B	✓	–	–

Sets the indentation of the first line of an element. This is most often used to create a tab effect for paragraphs, such as in novels and other printed books. Negative values are permitted, which cause hanging indents. Percentage values refer to the parent element's width. Care should be taken to leave enough margin for the hanging indent to be visible.

Examples:

```
P {text-indent: 5em;}
H2 {text-indent: -25px;}
```

text-transform

Values: capitalize | uppercase | lowercase | none

Default: none

Inherited: Yes

Applies to: All elements

Support:

	IE4	IE5	IE55	NN4	NN6	Op3	Op4
Win	✓	✓	✓	✓	✓	P	✓
Mac	✓	✓	–	✓	✓	–	–

Changes the case of the letters in the element, regardless of the case of the original text. The selection of letters to be capitalized by the value `capitalize` isn't a precisely defined behavior, depending as it does on words, which are difficult to define in a programmatic way.

If an element is set to `text-transform: capitalize`, only the first letter in each word should be uppercase, where a word is defined as strings of non-whitespace characters. For example, in the markup `antidis<span>establishment</span>arianism` only the first A should be uppercase, not the E at the beginning of the `span` element. Opera 3.6 incorrectly uppercases both letters.

Examples:

```
H1 {text-transform: uppercase;}
.title {text-transform: capitalize;}
```

vertical-align

Values:
baseline | sub | super | top | text-top | middle | bottom | text-bottom | *percentage*

Default: baseline

Inherited: No

Applies to: Inline elements

	IE4	IE5	IE55	NN4	NN6	Op3	Op4
Win	P	P	P	✗	✓	P	✓
Mac	P	✓	–	✗	✓	–	–

Sets the vertical alignment of an element's baseline with respect to the value of line-height. Percentage values refer to the line-height of the element itself. Negative percentage values are permitted and cause the element to be lowered, not raised.

Examples:

```
SUP {vertical-align: super;}
.fnote {vertical-align: 50%;}
```

---

white-space

Values: normal | pre | nowrap

Default: normal

Inherited: Yes

Applies to: Block elements

Support:

	IE4	IE5	IE55	NN4	NN6	Op3	Op4
Win	✗	✗	P	P	✓	✗	✓
Mac	✗	✓	–	P	✓	–	–

Defines how whitespace within the element is treated. normal acts like traditional web browsers: it reduces any sequence of whitespace to a single space. pre causes whitespace to be treated as it is in the HTML element PRE: with whitespace and returns fully preserved. nowrap prevents an element from line-breaking, as in the nowrap attribute for TD and TH elements in HTML4.

Examples:

```
TD {white-space: nowrap;}
TT {white-space: pre;}
```

---

width

Values: *length* | *percentage* | auto

Default: auto

Inherited: No

Applies to: Block elements and replaced elements

	IE4	IE5	IE55	NN4	NN6	Op3	Op4
Win	P	P	✓	P	✓	Q	✓
Mac	✓	✓	–	P	✓	–	–

Sets the width of an element. This is most often applied to images, but can be used on any block-level or replaced element. Percentage values refer to the parent element's width. Negative values aren't permitted.

Navigator 4.x applies width in an inconsistent fashion but appears to honor it on most simple text elements and images. WinIE4/5 applies it to images and tables but ignores it for most text elements, such as P and headings. Opera 3.6, weirdly, seems to set the width of images to 100%. but this is largely an illusion, since minimizing the window and then maximizing it again will reveal correctly sized images. Basic support information for the values of vertical-align is listed in the "CSS Support Chart" section.

Examples:

```
TABLE {width: 80%;}
P.sidebar {width: 20%;}
IMG.figure {width: 200px;}
```

---

word-spacing

Values: normal | *length*

Default: normal

Inherited: Yes

Applies to: All elements

Support:

	IE4	IE5	IE55	NN4	NN6	Op3	Op4
Win	✗	✗	✗	✗	✓	✓	✓
Mac	✓	✓	–	✗	✓	–	–

Sets the amount of whitespace between words. A word is usually defined as a string of characters surrounded by whitespace, but this isn't the case for many non–Latin-based writing systems. Indeed, there's intentionally no definition for "word" in the CSS specification. Length values can define a modifier to the usual spacing, not the entire space itself; thus, normal is synonymous with 0 (zero). Negative values are permitted and cause words to kern (bunch closer together).

Examples:

```
P.spacious {word-spacing: 0.5em;}
EM {word-spacing: 5px;}
P.cramped {word-spacing: -0.2em;}
```

CSS Support Charts

Browser compatibility—or lack thereof—is the biggest obstacle to adoption of CSS. The following browser support charts show how the most popular browsers support CSS on the Windows and Macintosh platforms. The browsers are Internet Explorer (Versions 3, 4, 5, and 5.5), Netscape Navigator (Versions 4 and 6), and Opera (Versions 3 and 4). The code is:

✓ Supported

✗ Not supported

P Partial support (some values are supported, some aren't)

B Buggy support (anything from a mangled display in the browser window to a browser crash)

Q Quirky support (browser is technically compliant but may not act as expected)

The charts are organized according to the CSS specification: basic concepts, pseudo-classes and pseudo-elements, the cascade, font properties, color and background properties, text properties, box properties, classification properties, units.

Each numbered note attached to the various charts refers to a correspondingly numbered section in the CSS1 specification. This specification may be viewed at *http://www.w3.org/TR/REC-CSS1*.

This chart and its notes are current as of January 2001. For the latest information, visit *http://style.webreview.com/*.

Basic CSS Concepts

Property or Value	Macintosh				
	N4	N6	IE3	IE4	IE5
Containment in HTML	P	✓	B	✓	✓
LINK	✓	✓	B	✓	✓
<STYLE>...</STYLE>	✓	✓	✓	✓	✓
@import	✗	✓	✗	✓	✓
<x STYLE="dec;">	B	✓	✓	✗	✓
Grouping	✓	✓	✓	✓	✓
x, y, z {dec;}	✓	✓	✓	✓	✓
Inheritance	B	✓	B	✓	✓
(inherited values)	B	✓	B	✓	✓
Class selector	✓	✓	B	✓	✓
.class	✓	✓	B	✓	✓
ID selector	B	✓	B	B	✓
#ID	B	✓	B	B	✓
Contextual selectors	B	✓	P	✓	✓
x y z {dec;}	B	✓	P	✓	✓
Comments	✓	✓	✓	✓	✓
/* comment */	✓	✓	✓	✓	✓

Notes

1.1 Containment in HTML @import

WinIE4+ imports files even when the @import statement is at the end of the document style sheet. This is technically in violation of the CSS1 specification, although obviously not a major failing; thus the Q rating.

1.1 Containment in HTML <x STYLE="dec;">

Navigator 4 has particular trouble with list-items, which is most of the reason for the B.

1.3 Inheritance

Navigator 4's inheritance is unstable at best, and fatally flawed at worst. It would take too long to list all occurrences, but particularly troublesome areas include tables and lists.

Windows95/98/2000							
N4	N6	IE3	IE4	IE5	IE55	Op3	Op4
P	✓	P	Q	Q	Q	✓	✓
✓	✓	✓	✓	✓	✓	✓	✓
✓	✓	✓	✓	✓	✓	✓	✓
✗	✓	✗	Q	Q	Q	✓	✓
B	✓	✓	✓	✓	✓	✓	✓
✓	✓	✗	✓	✓	✓	✓	✓
✓	✓	✗	✓	✓	✓	✓	✓
B	✓	P	✓	✓	✓	✓	✓
B	✓	P	✓	✓	✓	✓	✓
✓	✓	B	Q	Q	Q	✓	✓
✓	✓	B	Q	Q	Q	✓	✓
B	✓	B	B	B	B	✓	✓
B	✓	B	B	B	B	B	✓
✓	✓	✓	✓	✓	✓	✓	✓
✓	✓	✓	✓	✓	✓	✓	✓
✓	✓	B	✓	✓	✓	✓	✓
✓	✓	B	✓	✓	✓	✓	✓

1.4 Class selector

WinIE4/5 allows class names to begin with digits; this isn't permitted under CSS1.

1.5 ID selector

WinIE4/5 allows ID names to begin with digits; this isn't permitted under CSS1. All browsers apply the style for a given ID to more than one instance of that ID in an HTML document, which isn't permitted. This is properly an error-checking problem and not a failing of the CSS implementations, but I feel it's significant enough to warrant the ratings shown.

Pseudo-Classes and Pseudo-Elements

Property or Value	Macintosh				
	N4	N6	IE3	IE4	IE5
anchor	P	✓	B	✓	✓
:link	✓	✓	B	✓	✓
:active	✗	✓	✗	✓	✓
:visited	✗	✓	B	✓	✓
first-line	✗	✓	B	✗	✓
:first-line	✗	✓	B	✗	✓
first-letter	✗	✓	B	✗	✓
:first-letter	✗	✓	B	✗	✓

Notes

2.3 first-line

IE3 incorrectly applies `:first-line` styles to the entire element.

2.4 first-letter

IE3 incorrectly applies `:first-letter` styles to the entire element.

			Windows95/98/2000				
N4	**N6**	**IE3**	**IE4**	**IE5**	**IE55**	**Op3**	**Op4**
P	✓	✗	✓	✓	✓	P	P
✓	✓	✗	✓	✓	✓	✓	✓
B	✓	✗	✓	✓	✓	✗	✗
B	✓	✗	✓	✓	✓	✓	✓
✗	✓	✗	✗	✗	✓	✓	✓
✗	✓	✗	✗	✗	✓	✓	✓
✗	✓	✗	✗	✗	✓	✓	✓
✗	✓	✗	✗	✗	✓	✓	✓

The Cascade

Property or Value	Macintosh				
	N4	N6	IE3	IE4	IE5
important	✗	✓	✓	✓	✓
!important	✓	✓	✓	✓	✓
Cascading Order	B	✓	P	✓	✓
Weight sorting	B	✓	✓	✓	✓
Origin sorting	B	✓	B	✓	✓
Specificity sorting	B	✓	B	✓	✓
Order sorting	B	✓	✓	✓	✓

Notes

3.2 Cascading Order

There are simply far too many instances of NN4 problems to list here. If writing in support of NN4, make your style sheets as simple and as independent of cascading order as possible.

			Windows95/98/2000				
N4	**N6**	**IE3**	**IE4**	**IE5**	**IE55**	**Op3**	**Op4**
✓	✓	✓	✓	✓	✓	✓	✓
✓	✓	✓	✓	✓	✓	✓	✓
B	✓	P	✓	✓	✓	✓	✓
B	✓	✓	✓	✓	✓	✓	✓
B	✓	✓	✓	✓	✓	✓	✓
B	✓	P	✓	✓	✓	✓	✓
B	✓	✓	✓	✓	✓	✓	✓

Font Properties

Property or Value	Macintosh				
	N4	N6	IE3	IE4	IE5
font-family	✓	✓	P	✓	✓
<family-name>	✓	✓	P	✓	✓
<generic-family>	✓	✓	P	✓	✓
serif	✓	✓	✓	✓	✓
sans-serif	✓	✓	✗	✓	✓
cursive	✓	✓	✗	✓	✓
fantasy	✓	✓	✗	✓	✓
monospace	✓	✓	✓	✓	✓
font-style	P	✓	P	✓	✓
normal	✓	✓	✗	✓	✓
italic	✓	✓	✓	✓	✓
oblique	✗	✓	✗	✓	✓
font-variant	✗	✓	✗	Q	✓
normal	✗	✓	✗	✓	✓
small-caps	✗	✓	✗	Q	✓

5.2.2 font-family cursive

Despite a preferences setting for cursive fonts, Opera doesn't seem to apply the preference, but instead substitutes another font.

5.2.4 font-variant small-caps

IE4/5 approximates the small-caps style by making all such text uppercase. While this can be justified under the CSS1 specification, visually, it doesn't render the text in small caps.

Windows95/98/2000

N4	N6	IE3	IE4	IE5	IE55	Op3	Op4
✓	✓	P	✓	✓	✓	✓	✓
✓	✓	✓	✓	✓	✓	✓	✓
P	✓	P	✓	✓	✓	✓	✓
✓	✓	✓	✓	✓	✓	✓	✓
✓	✓	✓	✓	✓	✓	✓	✓
✗	✓	B	✓	✓	✓	✓	✓
✗	✓	B	✓	✓	✓	✓	✓
✓	✓	✓	✓	✓	✓	✓	✓
P	✓	P	✓	✓	✓	✓	✓
✓	✓	✓	✓	✓	✓	✓	✓
✓	✓	✗	✓	✓	✓	✓	✓
✗	✓	✗	✓	✓	✓	✓	✓
✗	✓	✗	Q	Q	Q	✓	✓
✗	✓	✗	✓	✓	✓	✓	✓
✗	✓	✗	Q	Q	Q	✓	✓

| | Macintosh | | | | |
Property or Value	N4	N6	IE3	IE4	IE5
font-weight	P	✓	P	✓	✓
normal	✓	✓	✗	✓	✓
bold	✓	✓	✓	✓	✓
bolder	✗	✓	✗	✓	✓
lighter	✗	✓	✗	✓	✓
100 - 900	✓	✓	✗	✓	✓
font-size	✓	✓	P	Q	✓
<absolute-size>	✓	✓	B	Q	✓
xx-small - xx-large	✓	✓	B	Q	✓
<relative-size>	✓	✓	✗	✓	✓
larger	✓	✓	✗	✓	✓
smaller	✓	✓	✗	✓	✓
<length>	✓	✓	B	✓	✓
<percentage>	✓	✓	P	✓	✓
font	P	✓	P	Q	✓
<font-family>	✓	✓	P	✓	✓
<font-style>	✓	✓	P	✓	✓
<font-variant>	✗	✓	✗	Q	✓
<font-weight>	✓	✓	✗	✓	✓
<font-size>	✓	✓	B	✓	✓
<line-height>	B	✓	B	✓	✓

Notes

5.2.6 font-size xx-small - xx-large

WinIE4/5/55 and MacIE4/5 all set the default font-size value to small instead of medium. (The exception is IE5/Mac when it's in strict rendering mode.) Thus, declaring an absolute font size (such as font-size: medium) almost certainly will lead to different size fonts in Navigator and Explorer. While this isn't incorrect under the specification, it's confusing to many people.

N4	N6	IE3	IE4	IE5	IE55	Op3	Op4
P	✓	P	✓	✓	✓	✓	✓
✓	✓	✗	✓	✓	✓	✓	✓
✓	✓	✓	✓	✓	✓	✓	✓
✓	✓	✓	✓	✓	✓	✓	✓
✗	✓	✓	✓	✓	✓	✓	✓
✓	✓	✗	✓	✓	✓	✓	✓
✓	✓	P	P	P	P	✓	✓
✓	✓	✓	Q	Q	Q	✓	✓
✓	✓	✓	Q	Q	Q	✓	✓
✓	✓	✓	✓	✓	B	✓	✓
✓	✓	✓	✓	✓	B	✓	✓
✓	✓	✓	✓	✓	B	✓	✓
✓	✓	P	✓	✓	✓	✓	✓
✓	✓	✓	✓	✓	✓	✓	✓
P	✓	P	P	P	✓	✓	✓
P	✓	✓	✓	✓	✓	✓	✓
P	✓	P	✓	✓	✓	✓	✓
✗	✓	✗	Q	Q	Q	✓	✓
P	✓	✓	✓	✓	✓	✓	✓
✓	✓	B	Q	Q	P	✓	✓
B	✓	✓	✓	✓	✓	✓	✓

Color and Background Properties

Property or Value	Macintosh				
	N4	N6	IE3	IE4	IE5
color	✓	✓	✓	✓	✓
<color>	✓	✓	✓	✓	✓
background-color	B	✓	✗	✓	✓
<color>	B	✓	✗	✓	✓
transparent	B	✓	✗	✓	✓
background-image	✓	✓	✗	✓	✓
<url>	✓	✓	✗	✓	✓
none	✓	✓	✗	✓	✓
background-repeat	B	✓	✗	✓	✓
repeat	✓	✓	✗	✓	✓
repeat-x	P	✓	✗	✓	✓
repeat-y	P	✓	✗	✓	✓
no-repeat	✓	✓	✗	✓	✓

Notes

5.3.2 background-color <color>

Nav4 doesn't apply the background color to the entire content box and padding, just to the text in the element. This can be worked around by declaring a zero-width border.

5.3.2 background-color transparent

Nav4 insists on applying this value to the parent of an element, not the element itself. This can lead to "holes" in the parent element's background.

Opera 4 has a bug that shows up only when a background has been repeated, and the rest of the background of the element is transparent (either by default or when explicitly declared). Scrolling the element offscreen and then bringing it back can cause "holes" to be punched through the repeated images of ancestor elements, thus creating visual anomalies.

			Windows95/98/2000				
N4	N6	IE3	IE4	IE5	IE55	Op3	Op4
✓	✓	✓	✓	✓	✓	✓	✓
✓	✓	✓	✓	✓	✓	✓	✓
B	✓	P	✓	✓	✓	✓	✓
B	✓	B	✓	✓	✓	✓	✓
B	✓	✗	✓	✓	✓	✓	B
✓	✓	✗	✓	✓	✓	✓	✓
✓	✓	✗	✓	✓	✓	✓	✓
✓	✓	✗	✓	✓	✓	✓	✓
P	✓	✗	P	✓	✓	✓	✓
✓	✓	✗	B	✓	✓	✓	✓
P	✓	✗	B	✓	✓	✓	✓
P	✓	✗	B	✓	✓	✓	✓
✓	✓	✗	✓	✓	✓	✓	✓

5.3.4 background-repeat repeat

WinIE4 repeats only down and to the right. The correct behavior is for the background image to be tiled in both vertical directions for repeat-y, and both horizontal for repeat-x. Nav4 gets this property correct on a technicality: since it doesn't support background-position, there's no way to know whether or not it will tile in all four directions if given the chance, or instead emulate WinIE4's behavior. Opera 3.6, MacIE4.5 and WinIE5 all behave correctly.

5.3.4 background-repeat repeat-x

WinIE4 only repeats to the right, instead of both left and right.

5.3.4 background-repeat repeat-y

WinIE4 only repeats down, instead of both up and down.

	Macintosh				
Property or Value	**N4**	**N6**	**IE3**	**IE4**	**IE5**
background-attachment	✗	✓	✗	✓	✓
scroll	✗	✓	✗	✓	✓
fixed	✗	✓	✗	✓	✓
background-position	✗	✓	✗	✓	✓
<percentage>	✗	✓	✗	✓	✓
<length>	✗	✓	✗	✓	✓
top	✗	✓	✗	✓	✓
center	✗	✓	✗	✓	✓
bottom	✗	✓	✗	✓	✓
left	✗	✓	✗	✓	✓
right	✗	✓	✗	✓	✓
background	P	✓	P	✓	✓
<background-color>	P	✓	P	✓	✓
<background-image>	P	✓	✓	✓	✓
<background-repeat>	P	✓	B	✓	✓
<background-attachment>	✗	✓	✓	✓	✓
<background-position>	✗	✓	P	✓	✓

Windows95/98/2000

N4	N6	IE3	IE4	IE5	IE55	Op3	Op4
✗	✓	✗	✓	✓	✓	✗	✓
✗	✓	✗	✓	✓	✓	✗	✓
✗	✓	✗	✓	✓	✓	✗	✓
✗	✓	✗	✓	✓	✓	✓	✓
✗	✓	✗	✓	✓	✓	✓	✓
✗	✓	✗	✓	✓	✓	✓	✓
✗	✓	✗	✓	✓	✓	✓	✓
✗	✓	✗	✓	✓	✓	✓	✓
✗	✓	✗	✓	✓	✓	✓	✓
✗	✓	✗	✓	✓	✓	✓	✓
P	✓	P	P	✓	✓	P	P
B	✓	P	✓	✓	✓	✓	✓
P	✓	✓	✓	✓	✓	✓	✓
P	✓	B	B	✓	✓	✓	✓
✗	✓	✗	✓	✓	✓	✗	✓
✗	✓	✗	✓	✓	✓	✓	✓

Text Properties

Property or Value	Macintosh				
	N4	N6	IE3	IE4	IE5
word-spacing	✗	✓	✗	✓	✓
normal	✗	✓	✗	✓	✓
<length>	✗	✓	✗	✓	✓
letter-spacing	✗	✓	✗	✓	✓
normal	✗	✓	✗	✓	✓
<length>	✗	✓	✗	✓	✓
text-decoration	B	B	B	B	P
none	Q	✓	✓	Q	✓
underline	Q	✓	B	Q	✓
overline	✗	✓	✗	✓	✓
line-through	✓	✓	✓	✓	✓
blink	✓	✓	✗	✗	✗
vertical-align	✗	✓	✗	P	✓
baseline	✗	✓	✗	✓	✓
sub	✗	✓	✗	✓	✓
super	✗	✓	✗	✓	✓
top	✗	✓	✗	✓	✓
text-top	✗	✓	✗	✓	✓

Notes

5.4.3 text-decoration none

According to the specification, if an element is decorated, but one of its children isn't, the parent's effect is still visible on the child; in a certain sense, it "shines through." Thus, if a paragraph is underlined, but a STRONG element within it is set to have no underlining, the paragraph underline still spans the STRONG element. This also means that the underlining of child elements should be the same color as the parent element, unless the child element has also been set to be underlined.

Windows95/98/2000							
N4	**N6**	**IE3**	**IE4**	**IE5**	**IE55**	**Op3**	**Op4**
✗	✓	✗	✗	✗	✗	✓	✓
✗	✓	✗	✗	✗	✗	✓	✓
✗	✓	✗	✗	✗	✗	✓	✓
✗	✓	✗	✓	✓	✓	✓	✓
✗	✓	✗	✓	✓	✓	✓	✓
✗	✓	✗	✓	✓	✓	✓	✓
B	B	B	B	B	B	B	B
Q	✓	✗	✓	✓	✓	✓	✓
Q	✓	B	✓	✓	✓	✓	✓
✗	✓	✗	✓	✓	✓	✓	✓
✓	✓	✓	✓	✓	✓	✓	✓
✓	✓	✗	✗	✗	✗	✗	✓
✗	✓	✗	P	P	P	P	✓
✗	✓	✗	✓	✓	✓	✓	✓
✗	✓	✗	✓	✓	✓	✓	✓
✗	✓	✗	✓	✓	✓	✓	✓
✗	✓	✗	✗	✗	✓	B	✓
✗	✓	✗	✗	✗	✓	✗	✓

In practice, however, setting an inline element to none turns off all decorations, regardless of the parent's decoration. The only exceptions are Opera and IE5/Mac, which implement this part of the specification correctly. Unfortunately, Opera 4 and Netscape 6 don't span inline images with the text decoration of a parent element. In addition, Netscape 6 appears not to use a parent element's decoration, but instead replicates it onto child elements, which is subtly wrong.

5.4.3 text-decoration blink
Since this value isn't required under CSS1, only Navigator supports it (surprise).

Property or Value	Macintosh				
	N4	N6	IE3	IE4	IE5
middle	✗	✓	✗	✓	✓
bottom	✗	✓	✗	B	✓
text-bottom	✗	✓	✗	B	✓
<percentage>	✗	✓	✗	B	✓
text-transform	✓	✓	✗	✓	✓
capitalize	✓	✓	✗	✓	✓
uppercase	✓	✓	✗	✓	✓
lowercase	✓	✓	✗	✓	✓
none	✓	✓	✗	✓	✓
text-align	P	✓	P	P	✓
left	✓	✓	✓	✓	✓
right	✓	✓	✓	✓	✓
center	✓	✓	✓	✓	✓
justify	B	✓	✗	✗	✓
text-indent	✓	✓	✓	✓	✓
<length>	✓	✓	✓	✓	✓
<percentage>	✓	✓	✓	✓	✓
line-height	P	✓	P	✓	✓
normal	✓	✓	✓	✓	✓
<number>	P	✓	B	✓	✓
<length>	B	✓	B	✓	✓
<percentage>	P	✓	B	✓	✓

5.4.5 text-transform uppercase

Opera 3.6 uppercases the first letter in each inline element within a word, which (according to the CSS1 Test Suite) it shouldn't do.

5.4.6 text-align justify

In Nav4, this value has a tendency to break down in tables but generally works in other circumstances.

Windows95/98/2000

N4	N6	IE3	IE4	IE5	IE55	Op3	Op4
✗	✓	✗	B	✗	✓	B	✓
✗	✓	✗	✗	✗	✓	B	✓
✗	✓	✗	✗	✗	✓	✗	✓
✗	✓	✗	✗	✗	✗	✓	✓
✓	✓	✗	✓	✓	✓	P	✓
✓	✓	✗	✓	✓	✓	✓	✓
✓	✓	✗	✓	✓	✓	B	✓
✓	✓	✗	✓	✓	✓	✓	✓
✓	✓	✗	✓	✓	✓	✓	✓
✓	✓	P	✓	✓	✓	✓	✓
✓	✓	✓	✓	✓	✓	✓	✓
✓	✓	✓	✓	✓	✓	✓	✓
✓	✓	✓	✓	✓	✓	✓	✓
B	✓	✗	✓	✓	✓	✓	✓
✓	✓	✓	✓	✓	✓	✓	✓
✓	✓	✓	✓	✓	✓	✓	✓
✓	✓	✓	✓	✓	✓	✓	✓
P	✓	P	✓	✓	✓	Q	✓
✓	✓	✓	✓	✓	✓	✓	✓
P	✓	✗	✓	✓	✓	✓	✓
B	✓	✓	✓	✓	✓	✓	✓
P	✓	✓	✓	✓	✓	✓	✓

5.4.8 line-height

Opera 3.6 applies background colors to the space between lines, as opposed to just the text itself, when the background is set for an inline element within the text. (See the CSS1 Test Suite for more details.)

5.4.8 line-height <length>

Nav4 incorrectly permits negative values for this property.

Box Properties

| | | Macintosh | | | |
Property or Value	N4	N6	IE3	IE4	IE5
margin-top	P	✓	B	P	✓
<length>	P	✓	B	P	✓
<percentage>	P	✓	B	P	✓
auto	P	✓	B	P	✓
margin-right	B	B	P	P	✓
<length>	B	✓	✓	P	✓
<percentage>	B	✓	✓	P	✓
auto	✗	✓	✗	P	✓
margin-bottom	✗	✓	✗	P	✓
<length>	✗	✓	✗	P	✓
<percentage>	✗	✓	✗	P	✓
auto	✗	✓	✗	P	✓
margin-left	B	✓	P	P	✓
<length>	✓	✓	✓	P	✓
<percentage>	B	✓	✓	P	✓
auto	B	✓	✗	P	✓

Notes

5.5.01 margin-top

All margin properties seem to be problematic, or else completely unsupported, on inline elements; see `margin` for details.

5.5.02 margin-right

All margin properties seem to be problematic, or else completely unsupported, on inline elements; see `margin` for details. Opera 4 sometimes applies right margins to all the boxes of an inline element, not just the last one. This seems to come and go somewhat randomly, but it's common enough to be easily noticeable.

			Windows95/98/2000				
N4	**N6**	**IE3**	**IE4**	**IE5**	**IE55**	**Op3**	**Op4**
P	✓	B	P	P	✓	✓	✓
P	✓	B	P	P	✓	✓	✓
P	✓	✓	P	P	✓	✓	✓
P	✓	✓	P	P	✓	✓	✓
B	B	P	P	P	Q	✓	B
B	✓	✓	P	P	✓	✓	✓
B	✓	✗	P	P	✓	✓	✓
✗	✓	✗	✗	✗	✓	✓	✓
✗	✓	✓	P	P	✓	✓	✓
✗	✓	✗	P	P	✓	✓	✓
✗	✓	✗	P	P	✓	✓	✓
✗	✓	✗	P	P	✓	✓	✓
B	✓	P	P	P	✓	✓	B
B	✓	✓	P	P	✓	✓	✓
B	✓	✓	P	P	✓	✓	✓
✗	✓	✗	✗	✗	✓	✓	✓

5.5.03 margin-bottom

All margin properties seem to be problematic, or else completely unsupported, on inline elements; see `margin` for details.

5.5.04 margin-left

All margin properties seem to be problematic, or else completely unsupported, on inline elements; see `margin` for details. Opera 4 sometimes applies left margins to all the boxes of an inline element, not just the first one. This seems to come and go somewhat randomly, but it's common enough to be easily noticeable.

Property or Value	Macintosh				
	N4	N6	IE3	IE4	IE5
margin	B	B	B	P	✓
<length>	B	✓	B	P	✓
<percentage>	B	✓	B	P	✓
auto	✗	✓	B	P	✓
padding-top	B	✓	✗	P	✓
<length>	B	✓	✗	P	✓
<percentage>	B	✓	✗	P	✓
padding-right	B	✓	✗	P	✓
<length>	B	✓	✗	P	✓
<percentage>	B	✓	✗	P	✓
padding-bottom	B	✓	✗	P	✓
<length>	B	✓	✗	P	✓
<percentage>	B	✓	✗	P	✓

Notes

5.5.05 margin

margin is fairly well supported on block-level elements in most browsers, with the notable exception of NN4.x. margin on inline elements is fully supported in IE5/Mac, IE55/Win, NN6, and Opera 4/5. margin should never be used on inline elements in NN4.x, which has severe and page-mangling bugs.

Opera 4's problems with correctly applying right and left margins to inline elements seems to get worse with margin.

Windows95/98/2000							
N4	N6	IE3	IE4	IE5	IE55	Op3	Op4
B	B	B	P	P	✓	✓	B
B	✓	B	P	P	✓	✓	✓
B	✓	✓	P	P	✓	✓	✓
✗	✓	✓	P	P	✓	✓	✓
B	✓	✗	P	P	Q	✓	✓
B	✓	✗	P	P	✓	✓	✓
B	✓	✗	P	P	✓	✓	✓
B	✓	✗	P	P	Q	✓	✓
B	✓	✗	P	P	✓	✓	✓
B	✓	✗	P	P	✓	✓	✓
B	✓	✗	P	P	✓	✓	✓
B	✓	✗	P	P	✓	✓	✓
B	✓	✗	P	P	✓	✓	✓

5.5.06 padding-top

All padding properties seem to be problematic, or else completely unsupported, on inline elements; see padding for details.

5.5.07 padding-right

All padding properties seem to be problematic, or else completely unsupported, on inline elements; see padding for details.

5.5.08 padding-bottom

All padding properties seem to be problematic, or else completely unsupported, on inline elements; see padding for details.

Property or Value	Macintosh				
	N4	N6	IE3	IE4	IE5
padding-left	B	✓	✗	P	✓
\<length\>	B	✓	✗	P	✓
\<percentage\>	B	✓	✗	P	✓
padding	B	✓	✗	P	✓
\<length\>	B	✓	✗	P	✓
\<percentage\>	B	✓	✗	P	✓
border-top-width	B	✓	✗	P	✓
thin	✓	✓	✗	P	✓
medium	✓	✓	✗	P	✓
thick	✓	✓	✗	P	✓
\<length\>	✓	✓	✗	P	✓
border-right-width	B	✓	✗	P	✓
thin	✓	✓	✗	P	✓
medium	✓	✓	✗	P	✓
thick	✓	✓	✗	P	✓
\<length\>	✓	✓	✗	P	✓

Notes

5.5.09 padding-left

All padding properties seem to be problematic, or else completely unsupported, on inline elements; see padding for details.

5.5.10 padding

padding is fairly well supported on block-level elements in most browsers, with the notable exception of NN4.x. padding on inline elements is fully supported in IE5/Mac, NN6, and Opera 4/5. padding should never be used on inline elements in NN4.x, which has severe and page-mangling bugs. Opera 3.6 honors negative padding values, which are illegal, but since you shouldn't use negative padding values, this is an easily avoided problem.

N4	N6	IE3	IE4	IE5	IE55	Op3	Op4
B	✓	✗	P	P	✓	✓	✓
B	✓	✗	P	P	✓	✓	✓
B	✓	✗	P	P	✓	✓	✓
B	✓	✗	P	P	Q	B	✓
B	✓	✗	P	P	✓	B	✓
B	✓	✗	P	P	✓	B	✓
B	✓	✗	P	P	✓	✓	✓
✓	✓	✗	P	P	✓	✓	✓
✓	✓	✗	P	P	✓	✓	✓
✓	✓	✗	P	P	✓	✓	✓
B	✓	✗	P	P	✓	✓	✓
✓	✓	✗	P	P	✓	✓	✓
✓	✓	✗	P	P	✓	✓	✓
✓	✓	✗	P	P	✓	✓	✓
✓	✓	✗	P	P	✓	✓	✓

5.5.11 border-top-width

Navigator creates visible borders even when no border-style is set and doesn't set borders on all sides when a style is set. Things get really ugly when borders are applied to inline styles. IE4 and IE5 correctly handle borders on block-level elements but ignore them for inlines.

5.5.12 border-right-width

Navigator 4.x creates visible borders even when no border-style is set and doesn't set borders on all sides when a style is set. Things get really ugly when borders are applied to inline styles. IE4 and IE5 correctly handle borders on block-level elements but ignore them for inlines.

			Macintosh		
Property or Value	**N4**	**N6**	**IE3**	**IE4**	**IE5**
border-bottom-width	B	✓	✗	P	✓
thin	B	✓	✗	P	✓
medium	B	✓	✗	P	✓
thick	B	✓	✗	P	✓
<length>	B	✓	✗	P	✓
border-left-width	B	✓	✗	P	✓
thin	✓	✓	✗	P	✓
medium	✓	✓	✗	P	✓
thick	✓	✓	✗	P	✓
<length>	✓	✓	✗	P	✓
border-width	B	✓	✗	P	✓
thin	✓	✓	✗	P	✓
medium	✓	✓	✗	P	✓
thick	✓	✓	✗	P	✓
<length>	✓	✓	✗	P	✓
border-color	P	✓	✗	✓	✓
<color>	P	✓	✗	✓	✓

Notes

5.5.13 border-bottom-width

Navigator 4.x creates visible borders even when no border-style is set and doesn't set borders on all sides when a style is set. Things get really ugly when borders are applied to inline styles. IE4 and IE5/Win correctly handle borders on block-level elements but ignore them for inlines.

5.5.14 border-left-width

Navigator creates visible borders even when no border-style is set and doesn't set borders on all sides when a style is set. Things get really ugly when borders are applied to inline styles. IE4 and IE5 correctly handle borders on block-level elements but ignore them for inlines.

			Windows95/98/2000				
N4	**N6**	**IE3**	**IE4**	**IE5**	**IE55**	**Op3**	**Op4**
B	✓	✗	P	P	✓	✓	✓
B	✓	✗	P	P	✓	✓	✓
B	✓	✗	P	P	✓	✓	✓
B	✓	✗	P	P	✓	✓	✓
B	✓	✗	P	P	✓	✓	✓
B	✓	✗	P	P	✓	✓	✓
✓	✓	✗	P	P	✓	✓	✓
✓	✓	✗	P	P	✓	✓	✓
✓	✓	✗	P	P	✓	✓	✓
✓	✓	✗	P	P	✓	✓	✓
B	✓	✗	P	P	✓	✓	✓
✓	✓	✗	P	P	✓	✓	✓
✓	✓	✗	P	P	✓	✓	✓
✓	✓	✗	P	P	✓	✓	✓
✓	✓	✗	P	P	✓	✓	✓
P	✓	✗	✓	✓	✓	✓	✓
P	✓	✗	✓	✓	✓	✓	✓

5.5.15 border-width

Navigator creates visible borders even when no `border-style` is set and doesn't set borders on all sides when a style is set. Things get really ugly when borders are applied to inline styles. IE4 and IE5 correctly handle borders on block-level elements but ignore them for inlines.

| | Macintosh | | | | |
Property or Value	N4	N6	IE3	IE4	IE5
border-style	P	✓	✗	✓	✓
none	✓	✓	✗	✓	✓
dotted	✗	✓	✗	✓	✓
dashed	✗	✓	✗	✓	✓
solid	✓	✓	✗	✓	✓
double	✓	✓	✗	✓	✓
groove	✓	✓	✗	✓	✓
ridge	✓	✓	✗	✓	✓
inset	✓	✓	✗	✓	✓
outset	✓	✓	✗	✓	✓
border-top	✗	✓	✗	P	✓
<border-top-width>	✗	✓	✗	P	✓
<border-style>	✗	✓	✗	P	✓
<color>	✗	✓	✗	P	✓
border-right	✗	✓	✗	P	✓
<border-right-width>	✗	✓	✗	P	✓
<border-style>	✗	✓	✗	P	✓
<color>	✗	✓	✗	P	✓
border-bottom	✗	✓	✗	P	✓
<border-bottom-width>	✗	✓	✗	P	✓
<border-style>	✗	✓	✗	P	✓
<color>	✗	✓	✗	P	✓

Notes

5.5.18 border-top

Opera3 doesn't apply border styles to table elements, which is the reason for the P rating. IE4 and IE5 don't apply borders to inline elements.

Windows95/98/2000

N4	N6	IE3	IE4	IE5	IE55	Op3	Op4
P	✓	✗	P	P	✓	✓	✓
✓	✓	✗	✓	✓	✓	✓	✓
✗	✓	✗	✗	✗	✓	✓	✓
✗	✓	✗	✗	✗	✓	✓	✓
✓	✓	✗	✓	✓	✓	✓	✓
✓	✓	✗	✓	✓	✓	✓	✓
✓	✓	✗	✓	✓	✓	✓	✓
✓	✓	✗	✓	✓	✓	✓	✓
✓	✓	✗	✓	✓	✓	✓	✓
✓	✓	✗	✓	✓	✓	✓	✓
✗	✓	✗	P	P	✓	P	✓
✗	✓	✗	P	P	✓	P	✓
✗	✓	✗	P	P	✓	P	✓
✗	✓	✗	P	P	✓	P	✓
✗	✓	✗	P	P	✓	P	✓
✗	✓	✗	P	P	✓	P	✓
✗	✓	✗	P	P	✓	P	✓
✗	✓	✗	P	P	✓	P	✓
✗	✓	✗	P	P	✓	P	✓
✗	✓	✗	P	P	✓	P	✓
✗	✓	✗	P	P	✓	P	✓
✗	✓	✗	P	P	✓	P	✓

5.5.19 border-right

Opera3 doesn't apply border styles to table elements, which is the reason for the P rating. IE4 and IE5 don't apply borders to inline elements.

Property or Value	Macintosh				
	N4	N6	IE3	IE4	IE5
border-left	✗	✓	✗	P	✓
<border-left-width>	✗	✓	✗	P	✓
<border-style>	✗	✓	✗	P	✓
<color>	✗	✓	✗	P	✓
border	P	✓	✗	P	✓
<border-width>	B	✓	✗	P	✓
<border-style>	P	✓	✗	P	✓
<color>	✓	✓	✗	P	✓
width	P	✓	✗	✓	✓
<length>	P	✓	✗	✓	✓
<percentage>	P	✓	✗	✓	✓
auto	P	✓	✗	✓	✓
height	✗	✓	✗	✓	✓
<length>	✗	✓	✗	✓	✓
auto	✗	✓	✗	✓	✓

Notes

5.5.20 border-bottom

Opera3 doesn't apply border styles to table elements, which is the reason for the P rating. IE4 and IE5/Win don't apply borders to inline elements, which is the reason for those P ratings.

5.5.21 border-left

Opera3 doesn't apply border styles to table elements, which is the reason for the P rating. IE4 and IE5 don't apply borders to inline elements.

N4	N6	IE3	IE4	IE5	IE55	Op3	Op4
✗	✓	✗	P	P	✓	P	✓
✗	✓	✗	P	P	✓	P	✓
✗	✓	✗	P	P	✓	P	✓
✗	✓	✗	P	P	✓	P	✓
P	✓	✗	P	P	✓	P	✓
B	✓	✗	P	P	✓	P	✓
P	✓	✗	P	P	✓	P	✓
✓	✓	✗	P	P	✓	P	✓
P	✓	✗	P	P	✓	Q	✓
P	✓	✗	P	P	✓	Q	✓
P	✓	✗	P	P	✓	Q	✓
P	✓	✗	P	P	✓	Q	✓
✗	✓	✗	✓	✓	✓	✓	✓
✗	✓	✗	✓	✓	✓	✓	✓
✗	✓	✗	✓	✓	✓	✓	✓

5.5.22 border

Opera3 doesn't apply border styles to table elements, which is the reason for the P rating. IE4 and Win/IE5 don't apply borders to inline elements, which is the reason for those P ratings.

5.5.23 width

Navigator 4.x applies width in an inconsistent fashion but appears to honor it on most simple text elements and images. WinIE4/5 applies it to images and tables but ignores it for most text elements such as P and headings. Opera 3.6, weirdly, seems to set the width of images to 100%, but this is largely an illusion, since minimizing the window and then maximizing it again reveals correctly sized images.

Property or Value	Macintosh				
	N4	N6	IE3	IE4	IE5
float	P	✓	✗	B	Q
left	B	✓	✗	✓	✓
right	B	✓	✗	✓	✓
none	✓	✓	✗	✓	✓
clear	P	✓	✗	✓	✓
none	✓	✓	✓	✓	✓
left	B	✓	✗	✓	✓
right	B	✓	✗	✓	✓
both	✓	✓	✗	✓	✓

Notes

5.5.25 float

float is one of the most complicated and hardest-to-implement aspects of the entire specification. Basic floating is generally supported by all browsers, especially on images, but when the specification is closely tested, or the document structure becomes complicated, floating most often happens incorrectly or not at all. The floating of text elements is especially inconsistent, although IE5 and Opera have cleaned up their act to a large degree, leaving WinIE4 and Nav4 the major transgressors in this respect. Authors should use float with some care and thoroughly test any pages employing it.

Opera 4 seems to place floated elements a little bit off from where the ideal place would seem to be, but in general, its support is extremely robust and can generally be counted on.

			Windows95/98/2000				
N4	**N6**	**IE3**	**IE4**	**IE5**	**IE55**	**Op3**	**Op4**
P	✓	✗	P	P	Q	B	Q
B	✓	✗	B	B	✓	✓	✓
B	✓	✗	B	B	✓	✓	✓
✓	✓	✗	✓	✓	✓	✓	✓
P	✓	✗	P	P	✓	B	✓
✓	✓	✓	✓	✓	✓	✓	✓
B	✓	✗	B	B	✓	✗	✓
B	✓	✗	B	B	✓	✓	✓
✓	✓	✗	✓	✓	✓	✓	✓

5.5.26 clear

Like float, clear isn't a simple thing to support. There is typically basic support, but as things get more complicated, browser behavior tends to break down. You should thoroughly test your pages when using this property.

Classification Properties

Property or Value	Macintosh				
	N4	N6	IE3	IE4	IE5
display	P	✓	✗	P	✓
block	B	✓	✗	P	✓
inline	✗	✓	✗	✗	✓
list-item	P	✓	✗	P	✓
none	✓	✓	✗	✓	✓
white-space	P	✓	✗	✗	✓
normal	✓	✓	✗	✗	✓
pre	✓	✓	✗	✗	✓
nowrap	✗	✓	✗	✗	✓
list-style-type	P	✓	✗	✓	✓
disc	✓	✓	✗	✓	✓
circle	✓	✓	✗	✓	✓
square	✓	✓	✗	✓	✓
decimal	✓	✓	✗	✓	✓
lower-roman	✓	✓	✗	✓	✓
upper-roman	✓	✓	✗	✓	✓
lower-alpha	✓	✓	✗	✓	✓
upper-alpha	✓	✓	✗	✓	✓
none	B	✓	✗	✓	✓

Notes

5.6.1 display inline

Opera 3.6 almost gets inline right, but seems to honor the occasional carriage return as though it were a <BR> element, instead of plain whitespace.

5.6.3 list-style-type none

MacNav4 displays question marks for bullets when using this value.

5.6.5 list-style-position inside

The positioning and formatting of list-items when set to this value are a bit odd under MacIE4.

Windows95/98/2000

N4	N6	IE3	IE4	IE5	IE55	Op3	Op4
P	✓	✗	P	P	P	P	✓
B	✓	✗	✗	✓	✓	✓	✓
✗	✓	✗	✗	✓	✓	B	✓
B	✓	✗	✗	✗	✗	✗	✓
✓	✓	✗	✓	✓	✓	✓	✓
P	✓	✗	✗	✗	P	✗	✓
✓	✓	✗	✗	✗	✓	✗	✓
✓	✓	✗	✗	✗	✗	✗	✓
✗	✓	✗	✗	✗	✓	✗	✓
✓	✓	✗	✓	✓	✓	✓	✓
✓	✓	✗	✓	✓	✓	✓	✓
✓	✓	✗	✓	✓	✓	✓	✓
✓	✓	✗	✓	✓	✓	✓	✓
✓	✓	✗	✓	✓	✓	✓	✓
✓	✓	✗	✓	✓	✓	✓	✓
✓	✓	✗	✓	✓	✓	✓	✓
✓	✓	✗	✓	✓	✓	✓	✓
✓	✓	✗	✓	✓	✓	✓	✓

Property or Value	Macintosh				
	N4	N6	IE3	IE4	IE5
list-style-image	✗	✓	✗	✓	✓
\<url\>	✗	✓	✗	✓	✓
none	✗	✓	✗	✓	✓
list-style-position	✗	✓	✗	✓	✓
inside	✗	✓	✗	Q	✓
outside	✗	✓	✗	✓	✓
list-style	P	✓	✗	P	✓
\<keyword\>	P	✓	✗	✓	✓
\<position\>	✗	✓	✗	Q	✓
\<url\>	✗	✓	✗	✓	✓

			Windows95/98/2000				
N4	**N6**	**IE3**	**IE4**	**IE5**	**IE55**	**Op3**	**Op4**
✗	✓	✗	✓	✓	✓	✓	✓
✗	✓	✗	✓	✓	✓	✓	✓
✗	✓	✗	✓	✓	✓	✓	✓
✗	✓	✗	✓	✓	✓	✓	✓
✗	✓	✗	✓	✓	✓	✓	✓
✗	✓	✗	✓	✓	✓	✓	✓
P	✓	✗	P	✓	✓	✓	✓
✓	✓	✗	✓	✓	✓	✓	✓
✗	✓	✗	Q	Q	✓	✓	✓
✗	✓	✗	✓	✓	✓	✓	✓

Units

Property or Value	Macintosh				
	N4	N6	IE3	IE4	IE5
Length Units	✓	✓	B	✓	✓
em	✓	✓	✓	✓	✓
ex	Q	✓	Q	Q	✓
px	✓	✓	✓	✓	✓
in	✓	✓	✓	✓	✓
cm	✓	✓	✓	✓	✓
mm	✓	✓	✓	✓	✓
pt	✓	✓	✓	✓	✓
pc	✓	✓	✓	✓	✓
Percentage Units	✓	✓	✓	✓	✓
<percentage>	✓	✓	✓	✓	✓
Color Units	P	✓	P	✓	✓
#000	✓	✓	B	✓	✓
#000000	✓	✓	B	✓	✓
(RRR,GGG,BBB)	✓	✓	✗	✓	✓
(R%,G%,B%)	✓	✓	✗	✓	✓
<keyword>	B	✓	✓	✓	✓
URLs	B	✓	B	✓	✓
<url>	B	✓	B	✓	✓

Notes

6.1 Length Units ex

All supporting browsers appear to calculate ex as one-half em. This is arguably a reasonable approximation, but it's technically incorrect.

6.3 Color Units <keyword>

Navigator generates a color for any apparent keyword. For example, color: invalidValue yields a dark blue, and 'color: inherit') (a valid declaration under CSS2) comes out as a vaguely nauseous green.

Windows95/98/2000

N4	N6	IE3	IE4	IE5	IE55	Op3	Op4
P	✓	P	✓	✓	✓	✓	✓
✓	✓	✗	✓	✓	✓	✓	✓
Q	✓	✗	Q	Q	✓	Q	✓
✓	✓	✓	✓	✓	✓	✓	✓
✓	✓	✓	✓	✓	✓	✓	✓
✓	✓	✓	✓	✓	✓	✓	✓
✓	✓	✓	✓	✓	✓	✓	✓
✓	✓	✓	✓	✓	✓	✓	✓
✓	✓	✓	✓	✓	✓	✓	✓
✓	✓	✓	✓	✓	✓	✓	✓
✓	✓	✓	✓	✓	✓	✓	✓
P	✓	P	✓	✓	✓	✓	✓
✓	✓	✓	✓	✓	✓	✓	✓
✓	✓	✓	✓	✓	✓	✓	✓
✓	✓	✗	✓	✓	✓	✓	✓
✓	✓	✗	✓	✓	✓	✓	✓
B	✓	✓	✓	✓	✓	✓	✓
B	✓	✓	✓	✓	✓	✓	✓
B	✓	✓	✓	✓	✓	✓	✓

6.4 URLs <url>

Navigator determines relative URLs in a style sheet with respect
to the location of the HTML document, not with respect to the
location of the style sheet itself.